RUNNING FROM THE LAW

RUNNING FROM THE LAW

WHY GOOD LAWYERS ARE GETTING OUT OF THE LEGAL PROFESSION

■

DEBORAH L. ARRON

1Ə TEN SPEED PRESS

TEN SPEED PRESS
P O Box 7123
Berkeley, California 94707

Designed by Elizabeth Watson
Typesetting by Lasergraphics, Seattle, Washington

Library of Congress Cataloging-in-Publication Data
Arron, Deborah L., 1950 -
     Running from the law / Deborah L. Arron.
          p. cm.
     Includes bibliographical references.
     ISBN 0-89815-413-8
     1. Practice of law—United States. 2. Lawyers—United States.
3. Law—Vocational guidance—United States.   I. Title.
     KF297.A87   1991
     340' .023'73—dc20   90-49559
                                                         CIP

Printed in the United States of America

          3   4   5   —   95   94

To

DAD

for leading me in

and to

MARK

for accompanying me out

ACKNOWLEDGEMENTS

My gratitude overflows for the support, inspiration, advice and encouragement of the following people:

All of the former and currently practicing lawyers, career counselors, and law school placement office directors who so generously volunteered their time for interviews;

Hindi Greenberg, originator of the Lawyers in Transition concept;

Jed Mattes, who helped me through multiple incarnations of the book's thesis and voice;

Jane Adams, Eugene and Irene Arron, Susan Cole, Judy and Mel Feinstein, Candy Lindner, Robin Low, Susan Molin, Perry Peterson, Cathy Rooney, Judy Schneiderman, Elizabeth St. Louis, Gerry Weinstein, and Susan Ziegman, all of whom were kind enough to read through drafts of the manuscript and give me invaluable feedback;

And Mark Jaroslaw, who edited, advised, listened, taught, shaped, prodded, pushed, and, most of all, accepted my ups and downs.

TABLE OF CONTENTS

◆

Preface/xi

◆

1: PRISON UNREST/1

◆

2: THE SCENE OF THE CRIME/5

An Insider's View: *Hindi Greenberg*. The Cell: *Stephen Feldman*. The Prison Walls: *Arnold Patent*. Partners in Crime: *Catherine*. The Bottom Line: *Richard*. Alibis: *Dennis*.

◆

3: THE RUNNER'S PROFILE/25

The Lawyer-Capitalist: *Bradley*. The Lawyer-Go-Getter: *Michael*. The Lawyer-Entrepreneur: *Rees*. The Lawyer-Integrator: *Earl*. The Lawyer-Super Woman: *Sharon*. The Lawyer-Peacemaker: *Linda*. The Lawyer-Altruist: *Kate*. The Lawyer-Humanist: *Norm*. The Lawyer-Crusader: *Ralph Warner*. The Lawyer-Visionary: *Arnold Patent*.

◆

4: UP AGAINST THE WALL/57

The Brainwashing: *David*. Lockstep into the Firms: *Elizabeth*. Following All the Rules: *Cindy*. The Ties That Bind: *George*. Golden Handcuffs: *Janna*.

♦

5: MAKING THE BREAK/75

Seeing the Light: *Barry*. Commuting a Life Sentence: *Bolling*. Plotting An Escape: *Robert*. Shock Therapy: *Valerie*. Scaling the Wall: *Mary Kay*.

♦

6: ASSUMING A NEW IDENTITY/93

Corporate. Entrepreneurial. Communications. Re-Education. Capitalizing on a Hobby.

♦

7: NO REMORSE/107

♦

8: COPING WITHIN THE LAW/111

Work Release Programs: *Robin*. Switching Sides: *Judge Smith*. Switching Cells: *Tom*. Furloughs: *Jon*. Recidivism: *Phil*.

♦

9: REHABILITATING THE SYSTEM/127

First Area of Improvement: *The Economics of Law*. Second Area of Improvement: *Collegiality*. Third Area of Improvement: *Legal Education*. Fourth Area of Improvement: *Civility*. Fifth Area of Improvement: *Emphasis on Mediation*. Sixth Area of Improvement: *Public Awareness*. In Summation.

♦

Epilogue/141
1991 Update

◆

Appendix 1: CAREER PLANNING TIPS FOR DISSATISFIED LAWYERS/145

The Evaluation Process. The Planning Process. Postscript to the Profession.

◆

Appendix 2: GETTING TOGETHER WITH OTHER LAWYERS IN TRANSITION/161

Finding Support. Suggested Career Assessment Format. Guidelines for Participation in the Workshop. Exercise #1. Exercise #2. Exercise #3. Exercise #4. Exercise #5. The Ideal Job Grid. Option Building through Group Brainstorming. Afterthoughts on Ideal Job Grid Brainstorming. Continuing Group Support.

◆

Appendix 3: WITH THE BENEFIT OF HINDSIGHT/179

Pre-Law Evaluation and Planning. Tips for Law Students and Recent Graduates. How to Develop Career Satisfaction as a Lawyer.

◆

Appendix 4: RECOMMENDED CAREER PLANNING RESOURCES/189

For Inspiration and Assistance with Career Planning. For Information about the Job-Finding Process. Exploring Alternative Positions in the Legal Profession. On the Psychology of Change. Career Counselors. Testing Resources.

◆

Footnotes/195

PREFACE

In life there are two tragedies.
One is not getting what you want.
The other is getting it.

♦

OSCAR WILDE

"One moment I'm certain that I cannot be a whole person and practice law. Then, overnight, I construct massive walls against doing anything else. It seems that I've walked out of the giant iron infrastructure into the big black void. Who am I? What do I want from life? Where am I going? Why did I leave my safe little prison for the frightening unknown?"

Those words are from my journal. They were written in the summer of 1985, soon after I had closed my law practice, withdrawn as a bar association leader, and turned my back on what promised to continue to be a prosperous professional future. In that journal entry is the genesis of *Running from the Law*.

Just before I left, I *appeared* to be doing very well. After 10 years, I enjoyed the luxury of choosing the types of cases I handled, and the clients I represented. Not only was I my own boss, but I was well-compensated enough to have accumulated a substantial investment portfolio. By automating and streamlining office operations, and lowering overhead, I had reduced the time I devoted to my practice to a reasonable 40-hour week and was taking regular vacations. Despite all that, I hated waking up to go to work.

Month after month, I struggled inwardly with my predicament, seeing no relief. No other form of law practice appealed to me at all. I

be a judge. No "sugar daddy" seemed likely to appear in
hadn't been trained to do anything else for a living. Finally,
......u to make use of some hard-earned savings to buy time off for
contemplation.

I was pretty certain I'd come back eventually. But the moment I
walked out of my office, I was flooded with an amazing sense of
excitement. Suddenly, my future was my own, and the possibilities
seemed endless. I felt unencumbered and all-powerful. With all those
positive feelings influencing me, it wasn't long before I began to toy with
the idea of turning my time-out into a permanent leave-taking.

Three months later, my elation surrendered to anxiety. No matter
how often my friends had criticized lawyers or the legal system, no
matter how much sympathy my family offered for my frustration and
fatigue, they all seemed strangely disappointed with my proposal.
"You're crazy to give it all up. What else will you do?" they wondered.
"You're a fair ethical attorney. We need you in the system," implored
others. Some simply shook their heads and said, "What a waste of the
last 13 years."

Instinctively, I knew that leaving the profession was the right choice
for me. Just the thought of returning made my stomach churn. But how
could I ignore the misgivings of the people who knew me best? Could
I be avoiding or overlooking some deeper inner turmoil by blaming the
legal system for my discontent? Answers to those questions continued
to elude me until two unrelated events occurred. First, several well-
respected Seattle attorneys suddenly quit *their* practices. And then,
while I mulled over this development, the phrase "running from the law"
popped into mind. Thus began the research phase of a book that would
explore why more and more good lawyers seem to be getting out of the
legal system.

My early interviews brought home the complexity of the phenomenon by raising a maze of questions: why did we leave the profession
while other attorneys — just as discontent — remain? Does gender have
anything to do with it? Or, are we otherwise temperamentally different
from those who stay? Did we ignore warning signs which might have
prevented us from leaving? Would resigning from our profession turn
out, in the long run, to be the best solution? Is this phenomenon among
lawyers reflective of a restlessness throughout society? Can changes be

made in the legal system to stop this flight?

Like any good investigator, I headed to the library. There, I discovered only two "state-of-the-profession" surveys and a few newspaper and magazine articles with any explanation of lawyer dissatisfaction, and one cryptic *ABA Journal* notation that described disaffected attorneys as "men never cut out to be lawyers in the first place, who have invested too much in becoming a lawyer to admit to themselves that they have failed."

Discouraged by the lack of media awareness, I turned to personal interviews with former practicing attorneys nationwide, law school career advisors and career counselors. I poured over U.S. Census and Labor Bureau statistics and tracked down a Harvard Law School study of career paths for lawyers. What emerged was a tendency among lawyers to cope with their unhappiness by switching jobs within the profession, or by leaving entirely. Still, I couldn't prove what I felt intuitively: that this trend toward dissatisfaction might be a harbinger of wider problems in the future.

Eighteen months after I began my research, the *National Law Journal* featured a front page article about attorney dissatisfaction. The "Baby Boomer" issue of the *ABA Journal* noted that "the best and the brightest [were] bored and burned out." A *Los Angeles Times* article asked why so many "highly trained and highly paid lawyers feel so low about their jobs." Similar articles appeared in such disparate publications as the Portland, Oregon *Daily Journal of Commerce, Crain's Chicago Business,* and the *Seattle Times.*

By this time, I had also discovered that two how-to books were in the works for attorneys considering job change within the profession; that an Oakland, California, attorney and a San Diego law professor were independently working on books about lawyer disaffection; and that an ex-practitioner from Cleveland, Ohio, had already completed a manuscript about lawyers who feel like "square pegs in round holes" in the profession. My conversations with some of these writers, and with many other current and former practicing attorneys, stoked my determination to complete my own study.

Shaped by my own bias as a former practitioner, *Running from the Law* focuses on abandonment of the profession as a lawyer's ultimate statement of disappointment with the way the legal system currently operates. That message comes through loud and clear from a diverse group of attorneys — those who no longer practice, those who are working their way out, and those who have found a way to cope with their discomfort within the profession. Most of the profiles in this book are anonymously presented to protect the privacy of those who agreed to talk to me. Some are further disguised by slight modification of their biographical data. Only those introduced with a surname disclose the interviewee's true identity.

Although I interviewed close to 100 different attorneys, and have read articles about or spoken informally with hundreds more, the ex-practitioners featured in *Running from the Law* are a carefully selected group. First, they all had "made it" in terms of professional respect and the skills they demonstrated. Although a few enjoyed their legal work, many of them were desperately unhappy with law at the time they chose to remove themselves to less stressful, more personally or financially rewarding environments. Many suffered lengthy, painful inner struggles in order to reach the point of departure. But all of them diligently searched for contentment within the profession before they decided to leave.

Therefore, *Running from the Law* is primarily an anthology of the insights and histories of courageous professionals whose choices make powerful statements about their values. The book is also my own catharsis. Almost four years after beginning my sabbatical, I have resolved not to return to the practice of law. My life is undeniably richer and more fulfilling as a result of that decision. Yet, even today, I occasionally reconsider my choice. Obviously, my personal exploration of this topic has not ended, and I welcome continued dialogue.

Deborah Arron
Seattle, Washington
May, 1989

xiv

RUNNING FROM THE LAW

Prison Unrest

Listen to your stomach, not to your head. Your head will rationalize you right into a job that you shouldn't have.

◆

RAY BRADBURY

Case One: *Barry* was a senior partner of one of America's most profitable law firms. After nearly 20 years in the profession, his law practice was stimulating, challenging, and lucrative and *Barry* had great admiration for his partners and employees. In his precious spare time, he actively monitored an investment in an art gallery and began to revive a youthful interest in painting. One day in 1981, while relaxing on a return flight from a case in Norway, *Barry* realized something startling about himself and his profession, and chose not to ignore it.

Case Two: *Mary Kay* dashed right up the ladder of success. As a prosecuting attorney in the 1970's, she was instrumental in designing and implementing a revolutionary method of handling sexual assault cases which soon became the national model. Before long, she was appointed chief criminal deputy of her office, the first woman in the county ever to hold that title. One day she received an invitation to direct a new clinical education program at a local law school. Soon after taking the post, *Mary Kay* had to restrain herself from shouting to her most talented students, "Don't do it. Get out while you can."

Case Three: *Bolling* entered the profession with impeccable credentials — Rhodes scholarship to Oxford University, Harvard Law School graduate, clerkships with Ralph Nader and a famed civil rights jurist — believing that there was no societal problem the law could not heal. Over the years, though, his understanding of the true nature of the legal

1

profession proved so disturbing that, in 1988, he resigned from his law firm, and from the practice of law.

Case Four: In 1983, *Janna* was a rising star at a prestigious Manhattan law firm. Based in Paris for two years, she played an integral part in a major international financial restructuring. To all appearances, she was securely on a fast track toward long-term stability and financial success. Inwardly, though, serious dissatisfaction with her profession was already incubating.

Although stories such as these are becoming more and more common among lawyers, it was not always so. Until recently, the choice to practice law, like that of medicine, presumed a lifetime commitment. Historically, only about six percent of all practicing attorneys ever abandoned the law.[1] The legal profession was so stable that most practitioners changed jobs within the profession only once during a 30- or 40-year career[2] (as compared to the rest of working America which reportedly changes careers every 10 years and jobs about every four).[3]

Today, though, lawyers are changing jobs at an escalating rate. Consider this:

- Three years after graduation from law school, only half of all young lawyers are still working in their first job in the profession.[4]
- Large law firms are experiencing the loss of up to one-half of each year's expensively recruited associates within three years,[5] as compared to an average stay of 25 years for those recruited in 1959.[6]
- Legal headhunters are prowling the profession in force, luring top-flight associates away from one, and into another, prestigious firm.
- More experienced attorneys are also making changes, affiliating with former competitors to gain more responsibility, client contact, compatible co-workers, freedom, free time, or just plain job satisfaction.

Individual job change, however, represents only a part of an overall restlessness within the legal profession. Law firm mergers, rare 10 years ago, are commonplace today. Solo practitioners and small firms are

2

joining forces to form specialty boutiques to compete with full-service megafirms. Entire departments are breaking away from their firms after accepting more lucrative arrangements from competitors. Like the Big Eight accounting firms before them, national law firms are spreading across the country by absorbing high-quality operations in other cities, or by opening branch offices. And, still other organizations of lawyers are coming together and separating as easily as pieces in a jigsaw puzzle.

Once a rare event, mobility among lawyers is now an accepted part of the legal environment. And with growing permission to change, more and more attorneys are questioning the very selection of their careers. The proof is found even among lawyers who purport to be satisfied with their jobs.

According to an American Bar Association survey, over 20 percent of those lawyers who report no overall dissatisfaction with their current employment still plan to change jobs in the next few years.[7] In fact, almost all practitioners report substantial dissatisfaction with at least one aspect of their employment, especially as it interferes with their personal lives.[8] Women have gained ground in the legal profession, but as a growing and visible minority, they are especially unsatisfied.[9] And, particularly distressing is the fact that an estimated half of all lawyers with five years' experience or less have come to regret their decision to enter law school.[10]

Other evidence of rising discontent among lawyers is being generated from a growing variety of sources.

- In 1988, the American Bar Association's annual meeting included a three-hour panel discussion on ways to cope with lawyer disaffection in the nation's law firms.
- In a 1988 survey of 1,000 Maryland lawyers, one third doubted they would continue to practice law.[11]
- A nationwide adult education program, the Learning Annex, now offers a course entitled "Lawyers and Legal Professionals: You're Not Stuck!"
- At People's Law School in Berkeley, California, a self-help law book publisher holds a well-attended weekend seminar called, "Let Me Talk You Out of Going to Law School."

- Within the last few years, both the *Washington Post* and the *Los Angeles Times* featured extensive articles about "lawyers who hate their jobs." New articles are appearing with greater frequency all over the country.
- In Philadelphia, LAWGISTICS, a company founded by a former practicing attorney to consult with law firms, quickly expanded into career planning for lawyers and now runs a second office in New York City to cope with the demand.
- A former Chicago practitioner whose career switch was featured in the *ABA Journal* and *Crain's Chicago Business*, and who was later swamped by inquiries, formed a thriving business called LAWTERNATIVES, which provides counseling and referral to lawyers who wish to explore new careers.
- A New York City career counselor who devotes 75 percent of her practice to attorneys, offers a career evaluation course for lawyers at New York University . . . and never has room for all of the people who want to attend.
- And, in San Francisco and Seattle, two fast-growing grassroot "Lawyers in Transition" programs are attracting to seminars and networking meetings hundreds of attorneys wondering how to take the next step in their work lives.

Significant uneasiness exists among this nation's lawyers. That fact is now well-documented. How that uneasiness develops, and where it can lead, will be demonstrated through the profiles that follow. Each individual history, and the narrative that accompanies it, will hopefully provide some insight and inspiration to others who are facing the same career and lifestyle choices. Taken as a whole, however, the stories in the following chapters represent something more significant. First of all, they prove that fundamental changes in the adversarial system, and the lawyer's role in society, are essential. And, more encouraging, they stand as evidence that momentum toward reform has already begun.

The Scene of the Crime

Lawyering in the U.S. simply isn't what it used to be.

♦

RALPH WARNER

Why would the four successful attorneys introduced in Chapter One — *Barry, Mary Kay, Bolling,* and *Janna* — turn their backs on a secure and profitable profession? Why are nearly 30,000 attorneys in the United States annually looking for jobs outside the practice of law?[1] What explains the fact that an estimated 41 percent of all practitioners — well over a quarter of a million lawyers — would willingly bail out of the profession tomorrow if shown a feasible alternative?[2]

Legal commentators agree that one contributing factor is the fierce competition generated by the astonishing growth of the legal profession in the last 15 years. To career counselors, the culprits are the stress and burnout that stem from the pressures of competition, the unpleasant professional interactions, and the never-ending deadlines, rules, and penalties that are so much a part of practicing law. Law school placement office directors point to yet a third factor: that liberal arts generalists buy into the illusion that a legal education will prepare them for a wide variety of fields and careers and then succumb to the pressure to take jobs in private practice. Among former practitioners, the adversarial role is the problem. To them, practicing law often translates into nothing more meaningful than transferring wealth from one person or institution

5

to another, documenting deals that have been put together by others, or finding intellectual solutions for controversies that occur at emotional levels. By combining the unique perspectives of these four groups, however, a clear conclusion emerges: that dissatisfaction among lawyers has taken root and grown because the legal system has become too crowded, close-minded, complicated and contentious.

AN INSIDER'S VIEW

Hindi Greenberg, the creator of the nation's first Lawyers in Transition self-help program, and one of the first practicing attorneys to speak publicly about lawyer dissatisfaction, is an able spokesperson for the frustration felt by other lawyers. Her point of view comes both from personal experience, and from listening to the complaints of several hundred of her peers. On the following pages, this San Francisco-based activist touches upon some of the reasons why good lawyers are getting out of the legal system.

◆

Hindi Greenberg's Profile

B.S., University of Minnesota, 1967
U.S. Army, civilian employee in Germany, 1967-69
J.D., Hastings College of Law, 1974
Judicial clerkships, 1974-76
Associate, large corporate law firm, 1977-78
Associate, small litigation firm, 1979-81
Litigation counsel, Bay Area corporation, 1981-84
Founder, Lawyers in Transition, 1985
Currently, contract attorney and director of San Francisco's Lawyers in Transition program

Greenberg's Statement: Lawyer dissatisfaction has been a taboo topic for a long time. The general public still looks suspiciously at lawyers who don't practice law. They wonder what's wrong with them; why they've "given up." The result is that lawyers feel pressure not to admit that they don't like their work.

6

People constantly tell me how much they appreciate what I'm doing. It's nice to be a star in that way; wonderfully ego-gratifying. But, I didn't set up Lawyers in Transition particularly altruistically. I just wanted to confirm that I wasn't crazy for disliking my work so much.

When I went to law school, it was with some idealism, and some naivete about what it was going to be like to be a lawyer. But who knew about all the little regulations and the nitty gritty? You get out of law school and all you have is theory, most of which isn't applicable to anything. What difference does it make if you understand the Rule Against Perpetuities or the Rule in Shelley's Case, when what you really need to know is how to file a paper with the court, write a brief, or argue a motion?

Law is a very strange, demanding profession. And, oh God, the paperwork! The literally thousands of pieces of paper: in some courts, the memorandum to set the case for trial; in others, the memorandum that the case is at issue; one paper to request a judgment, another paper setting forth the judgment, and yet *another* piece of paper which is the order for judgment. Plus, of course, more and more papers to cover your ass. The copies to the client. The fee agreements. A memo to the file of every phone conversation, and a copy of every letter, so that no one could question what you did or didn't do.

Even though I like detail, I hate the nonsensical detail required by the court systems. We once sent a pleading to an out-of-town court. It was sent back to us by the court clerk because we didn't put a blue paper on the back of it. We actually had to fly someone down that day to L.A. from San Francisco to file the pleading with *blue paper* so that we wouldn't be barred from court by missing the deadline date!

The trouble is, every court is its own fiefdom. There's no uniform system. From county to county, even within the same state, it's all different. And, there are so many unwritten rules that seem to be known only by those who have been around long enough in that court system to learn the etiquette.

The problem with the legal system is that it's law built on law built on law until you cannot understand the basic idea. New laws are passed, supposedly to correct the old ones, but which only make them more complex, and create the need for still more lawyers to be paid to interpret them or to find new loopholes. Cases are less often decided on the merits than on finances or tactics. I've seen too many times when somebody who doesn't have much money sues an entity big enough to afford one of the megafirms in town. The big firm sends three lawyers to a deposition, making it run two days instead of a few hours. The plaintiff has to settle because he can't afford to continue. That's just not right. Even worse, the merits of a case are often sacrificed for posturing, pressure and bullying. That really bothers me.

I hate to say that law is a completely negative profession. But it sure does make a point of looking for the downside of every situation. For example, you're drafting a contract for two people excited about going into business together, and you have to say, "Hold on. We have to look at what will happen if you break up." Or, you draft a prenuptial agreement, and have to talk about death and divorce, fighting over children and money, and relatives getting into the act. It's like walking into a house and saying, "Oh, what a beautiful new rug you have. Better tack down the corner so no one trips on it."

All jobs have their pressures and stresses. But practicing law seems to have more than its share of both. It's not only your clients' expectations that you can do anything, and will make everything right at the lowest possible fee. But also, your time frame is not your own. You get served with a motion that needs a response within a set period of time; or the court sends you a notice of a trial setting. You may have your schedule all blocked out, and all of a sudden someone slaps down an order for an emergency hearing to screw everything up. You cannot budget your time.

And that's the main reason why I'm now earning a living as a contract attorney. Once I accept an assignment, I have to give up some control of my time. But I still control when I work, or if I work at all.

THE CELL

No amount of money can adequately compensate lawyers for all the time they spend worrying about cases and clients, or for the night terror and anxiety attacks that haunt so many of them. The pressures of practicing law seem never to ease. Not only do attorneys constantly deal with the demands and expectations of others — clients, employers, judges, and opposing counsel — but almost every one of their actions is governed by a number of constantly changing rules, and the inflexible and unforgiving deadlines that control even more complex legal theories and government requirements. Says a partner in a San Diego law firm, "We have to run awful fast just to stand still." In this environment, even ordinary work days can seem like an endless series of term paper deadlines. Clearly, lawyers are working harder than they were a decade ago. "You have to if you want to be successful," says the managing partner of a Los Angeles megafirm.[3]

To compound the stresses, the nature of the adversarial system itself puts lawyers in a unique position. First, they're charged with the mission of trying to create agreement among hostile parties through the use of argument and advocacy. On top of that, no matter what they do, there's someone there to tell them they've done it wrong, or that they haven't done enough. No wonder, then, that the incidence of stress-related disorders in the lawyer population is among the highest of any professional group.[4] For example, studies have shown an unusually high percentage of practicing lawyers to suffer from depression,[5] and that the rate of alcohol abuse and dependency is nearly twice the national average.[6]

Stephen Feldman holds the right credentials to speak about the unrelenting stress experienced by practicing lawyers. Not only has he taught and practiced law himself, but, acting as a licensed psychologist now, he counsels attorneys-in-crisis and their families. On the following pages, he describes the many anxieties that plague the average practitioner.

9

Stephen Feldman's Profile

B.A., Duke University, 1960
J.D., Fordham Law School, 1965
Associate, small law firm, 1965-66
Associate, midsize law firm, 1967-70
Teaching fellow, Harvard Law School, 1970-72
L.L.M., Harvard Law School, 1972
Associate professor, University of Maine School of Law, 1972-78
Visiting professor, University of Nebraska College of Law, 1979-81
Ph.D., psychology, University of Nebraska, 1982
Currently, private psychology practice, adjunct professor of law and psychology, clinical assistant professor of medicine, and faculty member of the National Institute of Trial Attorneys

Feldman's Statement: Law was a tough thing to get up in the morning to do. I used to wake up and think, "Maybe, it's World War III and I won't have to go to the office. Maybe everything will be called off today."

For me, the anxiety started as far back as law school. I remember once sitting in a class, saying to myself, "I am paying attention, I have read the material, and I don't know what they are talking about. This is frightening." The only thing I could hold onto, I thought, was that I was fourth in the class and there were only three other guys who might be understanding it. If I was at the bottom of the class, I think I would have walked out.

I continued through law school like a little pigeon. I kept pecking, they kept rewarding me, and I continued to be a good student. I remember how tense law school was and how massive the work load seemed to be. The horrible news is that things are probably still that way for most lawyers, but they have just gotten used to it.

Stress is not just a matter of staying late at the office or becoming irritable at home. It is a serious business that can affect the quality and indeed the length of life. And, there are stresses peculiar to a lawyer's work.

First, practicing law is the only profession in which there is an

10

equal and opposite professional whose job it is to prove that you are wrong. A doctor does not ordinarily face a second doctor objecting to what he or she does. No opposing preacher is there to argue for the devil. The adversary system means there is little margin for error, as opposing counsel forever lurks, waiting to pounce on any mistake. Additionally, any error is forever part of the record, able to come back to haunt you long after you have retired to Hawaii and quit paying your malpractice insurance.

Besides opposing counsel, the work is often subject to criticism or praise by a third person, namely a judge or a jury. In law, someone wins and somebody loses. Judgments of your work are made virtually every day.

And, lawyers continually deal with the heavy responsibility of someone else's money, property, quality of life, family or even life and death. A lawyer faces these issues, and usually several client's problems, all in one day.

One lawyer described the essence of his practice as absorbing the client's energy. The client relieves himself of his stress by passing it on to you. You accept it from the client so the client can leave your office saying, "I feel better." That way, the client will be back.

The pressure never ends. One night, I was lying in bed reading a detective novel. I got to this steamy part that read, "Slowly, he ran his hand along Babs' thigh," and I suddenly found myself wondering, "Did I remember to file for an extension in the Babs Smith case?" Then it hit me, "I can't even read a dirty book without the law intruding."

Lawyers also continually deal with deadlines. Law is the business of deadlines, and woe to you if you miss that 10 days to file a notice of appeal (or is it 30?), the 20 days to answer a complaint, the statutes of limitations, the interrogatories, and so on and so on. There isn't an event that happens in a lawyer's professional life that doesn't have a time frame and a penalty attached to it.

Along with winning and losing comes conflict. The lawyer's professional life is filled with dispute, confrontation, and occasionally actual hatred. It is rare that a case will be pleasant; even adoptions can have snags. That unhappiness and conflict is reflected in the public's generally low opinion of lawyers as compared to other

11

professionals. This also adds to the stress.

And, you are the person expected to have the knowledge and expertise to give answers. Clients don't understand that you usually can't say either "yes" or "no," "black" or "white."

Being both a psychologist and a lawyer, I can speak to the difference in client attitudes. As a psychologist, when I call a client to make an appointment to come in, the response is usually pleasure in some form. It might be relief or gratitude. Almost always there is compliance. As an attorney doing the same task, there is usually hostility or suspicion. At the very least, there is apprehension, fear, tension, distance or coolness.

Similarly, when the phone rings for lawyers, it's like a time bomb going off. You can never tell what kind of crisis or attitude is going to come at you through the receiver. None of the phone calls may be actual Big Events. But just one may be, and it may be the next call.

I believe it's quite true that as people go forward in the practice of law they learn more and more about less and less. The legal profession is very narrowing to the soul. That's why lawyers need to get away and do something else; to discover there's a whole world out there that doesn't know there are two court systems. They need to remind themselves that the universe that has become so important to them is just a footnote in most other people's lives.

I once said to a nurse I was working with that I had found the secret to happiness in life.

She said, "Great, what's that?"

"What you have to do," I said, "is first figure out what you like to do and *then* figure out how to make money at it."

She thought for a minute, and then said, "I think that's prostitution!"

It was a great answer, but . . . I still think I had the right idea. It's the whole reason I went into psychology. I like to talk to people; I like to listen to people. Hell, if I like to do that, why not do it and make money too?

Most lawyers don't see their work that way.[7]

THE PRISON WALLS

The adversarial process, of course, is the foundation of the American system of justice. From the clash between two opposing viewpoints, fairness and truth are supposed to emerge. Furthermore, the system assumes that the two positions will be presented with equal persuasiveness and clarity, and that the arbiter exists in a vacuum, with no life experiences to color his or her thinking.

When confronted with conflicting opinions or a choice of actions, most people will gather information, mull it over, compare it to their own values and notions of right and wrong, and then decide with whom to side or what to do. Lawyers, on the other hand, know from the start what conclusion they must advocate. They then discover everything they can to support that position, and figure out everything they can to discredit the other side. By positioning people against each other, the adversarial system forces its servants to look at life's problems in unnatural ways.

Sometimes, disputes cut so closely to one's values or prejudices that they elicit a purely visceral response. Although lawyers often feel those same strong emotions, they are trained, and ethically obligated, to ignore anything that might sway them from zealous representation. To do so, they rely upon their intellects and, to a certain extent, set aside their humanity.

Arnold Patent accumulated 25 years of experience as a real estate attorney in an affluent suburb of New York City. Although his law practice was kind to him financially, he was plagued by a growing and undiagnosed physical pain; a pain he now attributes to the inner conflict he suffered working as a peacemaker in an adversarial system. Having closed his practice in 1980, Patent now lectures nationwide about achieving success in life by supporting others, rather than knocking heads with them. Here, Patent explores the foibles of the adversarial system.

◆

Arnold Patent's Profile

J.D., New York University Law School, 1953
U.S. Army, 1953-55
Solo practitioner, 1955-80
Real estate developer, 1978-80
Author, You Can Have It All, 1984, and Death Taxes and Other
Illusions, 1989[8]
Currently, seminar facilitator

Patent's Statement: The adversarial system is an anomaly; a dinosaur. It emerged out of the Middle Ages when people fought physically with each other. If they had a gripe or a disagreement, they took out weapons and beat each other up. The adversarial system was supposed to be an advance, but I don't agree with that. You can be so cutting with your mouth, or with your pen, that you can inflict far more lasting pain than if you had struck another person.

In an adversarial system, a lawyer does whatever he can to advance his clients' interests within certain very broad boundaries. Many times, the lawyer who represents the wealthier client can force the other side into submission just through the pre-trial practice of taking depositions and making motions. One side may be totally in the right, but the other side literally wears them out so that they never get to an equitable solution. My understanding of the system is that I was sworn to do just that, to gain my client every advantage I could.

The law presented major challenges to me early on because I had an underlying resistance to its assumptions. First of all, although the adversarial system purports to be definite and certain, or black and white, what you find is the gray. You learn how to change gray into black or white. How could I, as a lawyer, give my client an opinion or advice with any certainty when the system is inherently uncertain?

Letting the system work by one strategy or another never made sense to me either. A part of me wanted people just to tell the whole story and tell the truth. But, in the law, you can't ask certain questions; the rules of evidence prohibit it. I understood some of the overriding considerations, like not incriminating yourself. And yet, I felt the system was inherently so complicated that it didn't justify the higher purposes it was supposed to serve.

I was also taught as a lawyer not to let my feelings become involved. Since my father practiced law, I grew up with that belief. Everything was basically intellectual and logical. A part of me rebelled at this, and I had great difficulty suppressing feelings for my client, or his adversary, when one of the parties needed compassion.

There were also times when I couldn't do everything to advance my client's interests, and still trust that the other side would get adequate representation to balance that out. Very often it wasn't there. Either the other person could not afford counsel, or could not afford adequate counsel, so the match wasn't equal. The system purports to assume basic equality, but if you look out there, it is invariably unequal.

One of the practical problems you deal with when you get into the adversarial system is that you get caught up in its energy. As an individual, you become more demanding, more unreasonable and more uncompromising, just because you get into that adversarial mode. You become mostly ego. It's not only what's advancing your client's interests, but also "I'll show that guy. He ain't going to push me around."

I am constantly surprised at the things lawyers will do on a client's behalf. As a hired gun, the rules of etiquette and normal social behavior are suddenly gone. It's like driving in Los Angeles. You aren't an aggressive driver anywhere else, but you suddenly become an aggressive driver there just to survive.

PARTNERS IN CRIME

From 1970 to 1987, a period in which the U.S. population increased by less than 20 percent, *the number of lawyers more than doubled.*[9] These days, many practitioners agree that the tremendous migration into the profession transformed what used to be a profession that cultivated cordial working relationships into a culture where strangers do battle.

The American Bar Association looked at this issue in May, 1987. Paul Marcotte, a lawyer and reporter for the *ABA Journal*, discovered that "senior lawyers today generally shake their heads over a decline in professionalism. When [they] reminisce, there is a wistfulness about the way law was practiced even two decades ago . . . a time when lawyers generally knew their opponents and would frequently face the same lawyers in court."[10] In this more hospitable environment, most lawyers practiced according to an unwritten code which elevated the level of interaction to a gentlemanly etiquette. The written proscriptions found in statutes and court rules were relevant only to the rare hostile or emergency situation.

Nowadays, many attorneys are unfamiliar with the old code of honor. Instead, they narrowly interpret, and sometimes will even go as far as straddling the line of the written rules. If a court rule requires that they give five days' notice of a court hearing to the other side, that's how much notice they'll usually give . . . unless, of course, they can find an arguable exception which permits them to give less. As a result, a large percentage of court time is devoted to debates about whether an attorney has violated a procedural or ethical rule, rather than determining the basic issues of a lawsuit. And, where Atticus Finch, the gentle but effective lawyer in *To Kill A Mockingbird*, used to represent the preferred advocate, now a Rambo mentality has become more the norm, especially among litigators. Whether to boost egos or incomes, the development of good relationships with other attorneys has been forsaken in favor of convincing clients that they have hired a bigger gun than the other side.

In this environment, lawyers invite defeat if they are consistently accommodating. To cope, they become protean in their response — acting pleasantly when treated pleasantly; testy and belligerent when confronted with less courteous behavior. The result is that attorneys regularly take on the problems of 50 or 60 clients, and pursue many of them by knocking heads with equally contentious opponents. Sadly, combative interaction with others has become so much a part of their daily routine that many lawyers conclude that the average interpersonal relationship is grounded in conflict.

An attractive woman in her late 30's with a wry sense of humor, *Catherine* left the law to promote and direct animal welfare programs

16

after many years of volunteering for a local humane society. Eight years after she closed her law practice, *Catherine* can still remember with grim humor how being a lawyer contributed to her own unattractive metamorphosis.

◆

Catherine's Profile

B.A., University of Michigan, 1971
M.A., social psychology, University of Michigan, 1972
Associate editor, academic review journal, 1972-73
J.D., University of Michigan, 1976
Student legal advocate, 1976-77
Legal aid attorney, 1977-79
Solo practitioner, 1979-81
Currently, director of humane society

Catherine's Statement: All the time I practiced law I was angry. I was angry when my clients were evicted. I was angry when my clients were arrested (even though they were usually guilty). I was even angry when I managed to protect a client, or get a good result for one, because I knew that my clients needed money or a social worker a lot more than they needed me. Before long, I realized that practicing law was encouraging certain, maybe primal, anger in me. It encouraged me to be fairly pugnacious about almost everything. I wasn't sleeping well. I worried about my clients; but I worried more about losing.

The last case I handled in New York involved a client who bought a very expensive car that he couldn't pay for and then hid from the repossession agents. My colleagues and I scrutinized the paperwork and discovered not only Truth-in-Lending violations by the finance company, but also violations of the Debt Collection Practices Act by the collection agency. In the end, I got my client a free car. When I called to tell him about the settlement, he hardly seemed to notice. "Okay," he said, "now let me tell you about this other problem I have." I thought, "This guy isn't the least bit gracious; I just got him a free car." At the same time, it dawned on me that I didn't really care for my client, and I didn't really care that he

17

got a free car. I just liked beating the bank. I liked beating the bank a lot.

After that, I moved back to Michigan and opened a solo practice. I had lunch with a friend of mine from law school who I considered "politically correct" — you know, active, idealistic, a member of the Lawyers Guild. I realized that he had become cocky and self-absorbed, and I didn't like him anymore. Even more disturbing, I realized that a lot of what I didn't like about him was that he didn't give me a chance to talk about myself. And then I realized that I had also become cocky and self-absorbed. It's only now that I can see that the seeds of that egotism, and an obnoxious self-righteousness, were planted as far back as law school.

I remember representing, as part of a clinical education program, a black adolescent charged with burning down the Boys' Club. The police used tracking dogs to catch him, but I got him off. One week later he raped a 13-year-old girl. I was depressed for three or four months. But my clinical supervisor berated me. "Come on," he said. "Get with it. This is law. You were successful in representing him, not responsible." By the time I graduated from law school, I could see his point.

These days, I see many of my former classmates and associates operating in that kind of moral vacuum. It applies as much to their personal lives as to their work. They slip in and out of relationships; they avoid personal responsibility. Fortunately, I was conscious of the person I had become as an attorney, and got out in time.

THE BOTTOM LINE

The profession's astonishing population growth has also forced more lawyers to compete for a limited pool of business. As a result, lawyers and law firms are emphasizing the bottom line like never before.

Twenty to 30 years ago, a law practice was an uncomplicated, low-budget operation. "All you really needed to practice law was an office, a desk, a lawyer, a secretary, a table and pencil, and a law book or two," contends Richard P. Reed, practicing attorney and author of *Managing a Law Practice: The Human Side*.[11] "The invested capital was relatively low in proportion to the total fee revenue and the components of overhead low enough to be included in whatever the lawyer decided was an appropriate fee." Determining an appropriate fee was an equally simple task. According to Reed, "You reviewed the file, hefted it, and then by intuition sent a statement 'for services rendered.'" That is, "until someone discovered that lawyers who kept time records earned more than those who did not."[12] Now, the hourly billing system is the foundation of legal economics.

Reliance upon the hourly billing system has gradually reduced the likelihood that attorneys will make good money practicing law. First of all, billing by the hour confers the highest rewards on attorneys who turn small problems into big cases. Then, the effects of inflation on fixed operating costs and the expense of running a technologically-equipped law office force lawyers to raise their hourly rates higher and higher in order to maintain their incomes. The result is that "legal services often are overpriced or underpriced, but rarely accurately or competitively priced," according to William C. Cobb, a management consultant to the legal profession. Worse yet, "sophisticated clients understand that hours worked don't necessarily equate to value — to the competitive and economic disadvantage of a law firm."[13]

Because hourly fees bear too little relationship to the value of the services rendered, clients decide to avoid lawyers rather than take the chance of getting gouged by their inefficiency. Small business owners, regarding lawyers as sure deal-killers, now often seal agreements with handshakes. Or, they might copy simple contractual language from documents used in previous deals, or from mass-produced forms. Many lay persons accomplish such routine matters as uncontested divorces and relatively uncomplicated estate planning with the assistance of do-it-yourself books, self-help courses and quasi-legal organizations. Because lawyers cannot handle these types of matters at a competitive price, they forfeit what used to be the "bread and butter" of a law practice. Moreover, competition from the glut of attorneys for a smaller pool of potential clients prevents attorneys from raising their hourly rates enough to counteract the forces of inflation. As a result, although the most elite and well-managed law firms are paying millions of dollars to a few partners,[14] the business of law overall has become less profitable in the last 10 years.[15]

Firms have responded to these recent market forces by applying the red pencil to hiring, firing, expansion and partnership decisions, and by upping the billable hour requirements of their partners and associates to levels only workaholics and obsessive-compulsives can meet. At the same time, these same firms have imposed a severe penalty for failing to meet those expectations. The Manhattan custom of hiring many more associates than will become partners — once considered mean-spirited and unnecessary in other cities — has become the norm. In another example of cost-cutting, some firms have abandoned partnership-track associate positions in favor of contract employees. They bring attorneys aboard who negotiate year-by-year employment agreements with the understanding that their jobs will never become permanent. More and more, the law has changed from a gentleman's profession to big business. And, from that perspective, lawyers are not professional colleagues as much as easily replaceable inventory.

The market adjustments in the legal profession have been a focus, a fascination, and even a livelihood for one former practitioner. After 10 years searching for a niche in the profession, *Richard* now teaches law firms more effective ways to manage their staffs, to compete in the marketplace, to communicate with clients and juries, and how to pick and choose attorneys who will fit into and enhance the overall work environment. The largest part of his practice, however, consists of counseling dissatisfied attorneys about their options in and outside of law. From this perch, *Richard* has studied the impact of changing economic forces on lawyers and the legal profession.

♦

Richard's Profile

B.A., Syracuse University, 1969
J.D., University of Pennsylvania Law School, 1972
Assistant attorney general, 1972-74
Legal aid lawyer, 1974-76
Associate, 10-attorney firm, 1976-79
Theatrical negotiator, 1979
Solo practitioner, 1980-83
Currently, career counselor and consultant to lawyers

Richard's Statement: Fifteen or 20 years ago, law was a professional culture where you joined a firm, worked your way up to partnership over five to eight years, became a partner, and then stayed with that firm forever. There was an assumption that if a firm hired you as an associate, and you didn't screw up, you would make partner. Business was obtained through networking and through clubs, civic associations and just being a prominent citizen. Trust and loyalty were so high that clients gave lawyers blank checks to represent them. A whole culture grew up believing lawyers were not in "business," but were part of a noble profession.

Nowadays, clients no longer feel allegiance to one law firm. For each separate transaction, they hunt for expertise at the most reasonable price. And as they take their business elsewhere, a firm's mix of cases changes rapidly. It makes it harder to predict manpower needs and most law firms end up underhiring and overworking associates. Added to that is increased economic pressure from the high cost of the technology that is essential to a law office today — computers, word processing gear, laser printers, cost accounting, high-speed photocopiers, FAX machines.

Because of competition for clients and for well-credentialed associates; because of the profit squeeze from the high cost of technology; because of the change in corporate management, law firms are feeling more pressure to run less like clubs and more like efficient businesses. When a firm wants to expand because marketing needs dictate it, it buys up or merges with another practice. Employment decisions are based purely on economic considerations, such as the

21

kind of associate-to-partner ratio needed to maintain cash flow. When a partner no longer brings in a lot of business, pressure is exerted to push him out, retire him early, or dissolve the partnership. Lawyers are hired, paid and traded like baseball players. Associates have become fungible commodities instead of potential partners.

Now, a law school graduate who says, "Law is what I've always wanted to do and I plan to do it for the next 40 or 50 years," is finding it much harder to set a long-term course in the profession.

ALIBIS

Although the adversarial system was originally designed to resolve disputes without resorting to violence, the application of increasingly complex legal theories to even more complex factual situations has produced what often appears to be a hodgepodge of illogical decisions held together by cumbersome procedural rules. As the end of this century nears, the intent of the system has been further eroded by growing government regulation, strict legislative requirements, clever lawyering, the pressures of competition, and, blunt as it seems, greed. What used to be a gentleman's profession, relying upon a code of honor more stringent than the Rules of Professional Conduct, has today degenerated into a hostile and unstable setting.

No matter how uncomfortable the working environment has become, though, monetary considerations have turned dissatisfaction into a major predicament for most lawyers. Financially struggling practitioners doubt their ability to succeed in arenas outside law because of their lack of success as lawyers. On the other hand, many successful attorneys feel tied to lawyering by "golden handcuffs." They're so caught up in the lifestyle their high incomes buy for themselves and their families that they suppress their yearnings for more fulfilling work. In this way, unhappy lawyers all serve time within one of our society's most elegantly appointed prisons.

Yet if they want to run from the law, these same lawyers are often branded as losers or misfits by their more complacent peers. Some law firms go so far as to isolate attorneys who question the value of their employment, seeking to prevent their complaints from infecting the attitudes of their co-workers. An *ABA Journal* article, in fact, blamed flight from the law on the decline of institutional loyalty and the escalation of self-interest, as if there was something wrong with lawyers who bail out of their profession when they "do not get what they want from law, or if it seems to be a dead end."[16] What follows, according to one ex-practitioner, is a "conspiracy of silence"[17] about dissatisfaction with the profession.

Working from the inside, attorneys are probably the best positioned to reform what has become an outmoded, and too often ineffective, framework for order and justice. But, there are those like *Dennis* who believe that current practitioners are also the least motivated to do anything about it.

◆

Dennis' Profile

B.A., University of Washington, 1972
J.D., Georgetown University Law School, 1975
Deputy prosecuting attorney, 1975-83
Masters in film, University of Southern California, 1986
Freelance scriptwriter and part-time law clerk, 1986-1988
Currently, practicing attorney

Dennis' Statement: In this country, the law works much better for lawyers than it does for anybody else. It just does. We lawyers are making wonderful livings off other people's discomfort, woe and pain because that is how we have decided it should work. In Los Angeles County, you don't get a case to trial until five years after it's filed, and then only because of a rule *requiring* cases to be brought to trial within five years. Either the lawyers push it off because it ceases to be a priority until four years have gone by, or the court administrators say, "Hey, look at all these other cases approaching their five-year limit. You go behind them." That's just scandalous. You get involved in an automobile accident and you don't know whether you will see a dime of compensation for five years. Whatever happened to justice delayed being justice denied?

But if you talk to most lawyers they say, "Yeah, I guess you're probably right. Nothing we can do about it though."

I was in Georgetown Law School at a time when universities were being shut down, and people were very upset about the Vietnam War. But you never heard the students or faculty members apply that same kind of creative attitude to the legal system. I never heard, "Gee, let's do something about the law. Let's make the law better." Right from law school, lawyers in this country are prepared to accept the law as it's currently practiced as being the only way it can be practiced.

Why can't we look for solutions to this inequity instead of building a system that is great for lawyers and not so good for other people? It's a scandal.

The Runner's Profile

To destroy is always the first step in any creation.

◆

e. e. cummings

D rop-outs from the legal profession share a disturbing secret: something is terribly wrong with the way law is practiced today. Over and over again, these ex-practitioners complain that the legal system is not only not *meaningful* to their lives, but, all too often, does not support those it intends to serve, or is counterproductive to the real needs of society.

The complaints come as readily from corporate lawyers as from counterculture activists; as often from business attorneys as criminal prosecutors and defenders. Even those whose departure was motivated by an interest in another field, admit that what spurred them was a basic dissatisfaction with the lawyer's lifestyle and working environment.

Former corporate lawyers contend legal work wastes resources, costs too much money, and doesn't generate enough profits to justify the time and effort involved. Litigators find themselves bogged down in procedural requirements, unproductive paper pushing, and settlements that merely massage conflicts or, worse, aggravate them. Billable hour requirements and the need to respond to the unnecessary actions of their opponents consume all of their time and energy. Lawyers with children, especially, resent their professional demands; they worry about devoting more time to their families at the expense of forward movement in their careers.

Ex-practitioners also fault contemporary economics for eroding what used to be an honorable profession. Those who entered the law to "do good," or to bring peace to the lives of those in conflict, are often demoralized by their "hired gun" role, and crave more cordial and constructive relationships with clients and colleagues. At another level, a subtle pressure to discard their values finally wears them down. "I was taught that a good lawyer can advocate any position; only a poor lawyer chooses sides," contends Hindi Greenberg, founder of Lawyers in Transition. "But if that is so, then a good lawyer must be like a prostitute, who works well for anyone who pays."

What compounds these frustrations is an apparent powerlessness to effect change. Creative types, who rejoice in novel solutions to old problems, complain of being frustrated as the law inches toward change by piling one precedent and rule atop another. Those who stormed law school to save the world run into a ponderous and reactionary system that, especially in the last 10 years, seems to have done little for mankind. "That was the cruelest thing about the law experience. It was a hoax," asserts ex-practitioner Ralph Warner, now co-owner and editor of Berkeley's Nolo Press, a "do-it-yourself" law book publishing house. "What is going to change America's view of poverty?" asks Warner. "It's certainly not going to be some lawyer filing an endless 227-page brief about why the Fourteenth Amendment says there shouldn't be soup kitchens."

Lastly, some ex-practitioners consider the adversarial system counter-productive to an Aquarian society. To them, law's essential nature pits one against another in a process that separates and divides, while they would rather see mankind joining together to create a more peaceful, productive world.

Although most ex-practitioners can cite a variety of motivations for their move, one theme for each seems to emerge most strongly. On the following pages, the 10 most common categories of complaint are profiled — The Capitalist, Go-Getter, Entrepreneur, Integrator, Super Woman, Peacemaker, Altruist, Humanist, Crusader, and Visionary. Taken as a whole, they present a complete picture of the distress experienced by so many lawyers.

THE LAWYER-CAPITALIST

Lawyer-Capitalists do their best to escape the economic confines of the legal system's hourly billing system. Motivated by a desire to realize more income for each hour of their labor, they cash in on their years of legal experience to propel themselves into more prestigious and lucrative positions outside the profession.

Once they leave, however, they gain a new perspective on the value of legal work. Because most lawyers bill by the hour, the more time they spend, the more money they earn. Lawyers therefore can be compensated for running down dead ends, taking actions which enlarge disputes, and even for papering their files to prove what they did or did not do in case of a subsequent claim of professional negligence. Most clients (the exceptions being corporations with in-house legal staffs to oversee the work of outside counsel) have no way of evaluating or controlling how their attorneys spend their money. Unnecessary actions and inefficient work habits are therefore rewarded even though the clients' bottom-line objectives might be ignored. In fulfilling the charge to "complicate, keep a dispute alive, and make everything technical,"[1] the Lawyer-Capitalists come to realize, and later will admit, that much legal work is a waste of time, money and effort.

Bradley is one Lawyer-Capitalist who took the conventional path into the legal profession. After successfully practicing as a litigator of complex corporate disputes for almost 20 years, he left for a management position in a major corporation. As an outsider looking in, *Bradley* now has a much different fix on the value of legal work, and the state of the profession, than he did in his previous employment.

◆

Bradley's Profile

B.A., Stanford University, 1965
J.D., Yale Law School, 1968
Litigation partner, national megafirm, 1968-87
Currently, senior vice-president of a Fortune 500 corporation

Bradley's Statement: As in any service business, the greatest constraint on a practicing lawyer is time. With competition limiting how high hourly rates can go, and with operating costs rising and profit margins narrowing, the goal becomes to bill more and more hours. But with that comes a never-ending rat race. I mean, there are only so many hours in a day. And, it's a constant temptation to spend all of them practicing law.

That was one of the biggest detriments of the profession. I spent so much of my time practicing law that I was not able to spend enough of it on the rest of my life, my family, my hobbies — pursuing interests that would have kept me from being a completely dull, glazed soul, able to talk only about law.

The time system of billing is simply not in the legal profession's long-term interest. As lawyers accumulate experience and get better at their jobs, they end up spending fewer hours doing the work and can cost their clients less even though their judgment is worth a lot more. Then, as they invest in expensive technology which produces their work even faster, they end up passing the benefit of that additional efficiency along to the client as well. Another method of billing — perhaps a flat fee for services in the medical profession's model, or the "lump-sum job" arrangement of engineers — would allow lawyers to retain the benefits of their expertise. But if they want to stop working like wage-hour slaves, they have to get past their risk-averse mentality.

An awful lot of lawyers are scratching out there, and I think it causes them to engage in excesses they might not engage in if life were a little easier. For example, lawsuits are brought that shouldn't be brought. Divorce lawyers often look only at how much they can make out of the divorce, rather than how they can get it resolved without disrupting lives that already are in considerable turmoil.

I don't think that's consistent with the calling of the legal profession, but beauty, after all, is in the eye of the beholder. There are clients who talk about the lawyer's obligation to serve society, but want their mean, tough trial lawyer to look out for them when they have a problem. So, in a sense, lawyers are simply responding to what they perceive the client wants.

I remember one case in particular in which our client, who was being sued, had a very weak defense. We tried to convince him to settle the case before trial, but it was to no avail. Instead, we ended up losing it miserably. The client blamed the loss on our representation and brought in another well-known practitioner to handle the appeal. That lawyer told the client, "By God, we are going to turn this around," even though he didn't have a chance in hell of winning. The client needed salvation, and he followed that lawyer like Oral Roberts. Eventually, at great expense to the client, they lost the appeal. At that point, the lawyer told the client that the judge was biased and clearly didn't understand the case. The client loved the lawyer. All he wanted was somebody to assure him that he was right.

Sometimes clients take your advice; sometimes they don't. When they don't, it's their money that's at risk. That's a major difference between being a businessman and practicing law. Whatever you do in law, it's always the client's money that gets spent. That fact, combined with the demands of the hourly billing system, contribute to a lot of unnecessary work by lawyers.

Here's another example. Last year we had about six different law firms involved in a leveraged lease transaction. All of them insisted on changing things (which didn't make any substantive difference) so that our printing bill ended up exceeding the bill of almost every one of the seven lawyers who were involved. And the money was wasted. No one will ever read those documents. The leases are too convoluted and too complex by a factor of five. The lawyers spent mind-boggling amounts of time correcting things and changing words that were not ever going to have any effect on the transaction.

The thoughtful, reflective, mature, experienced judgment of some lawyers is worth the money. What is not worth the price are all the frills — the documentation, the extraordinarily expensive research, the hoards of paralegals, the endless discovery in litigation to ferret out proof of facts that you know or suspect from the beginning; constantly doing battle, trying to best the other guy rather than put something together.

Overall, I'd say that lawyers tend to do more than is necessary and to cost more than they are worth.

THE LAWYER GO-GETTER

Lawyer Go-Getters — for the most part, trial attorneys — enter the legal profession for the opportunity to perform, and for the emotional high of winning big. "It was fabulous in the beginning," exclaimed *Jerry*, for 14 years a criminal defense attorney in Oakland, California. "I played out the childhood fiction of what I saw on TV. I acted in a non-scripted drama, and it was very satisfying." Go-Getters thrive on the competition and theatrics of the courtroom, while despising the tedium of office work. Basically, they love winning and hate losing.

Go-Getters consciously choose litigation as an outlet for their energy and their need to interact with others. But the days are over when trial work can fully satisfy the personable, action-oriented lawyers. Modern litigation wages "paper wars," marshalling paralegals, motions and strategies in a grand attack that usually ends with an anticlimactic settlement on the courthouse steps. Lawsuits have become wars of attrition, one side wearing the other down with tedious stacks of interrogatories, inconsequential motions before uninterested judges, and interminable examinations of witnesses about unexciting elements of their ordinary lives.

In order to be competent and effective, the Lawyer Go-Getters more often sit behind desks in climate-controlled offices than get out into the public eye. For Go-Getters like *Michael*, the decision to leave the law comes only after spending enough time in the profession to realize that experiencing the rush of winning a big case happens so infrequently that it cannot possibly overcome the boredom of preparing for it. As an M.B.A. candidate in Chicago, *Michael* now waits to get into the business world to make what he hopes will be a bigger difference than what he achieved through lawyering.

◆

Michael's Profile

B.A., Colorado College, 1975
J.D., University of Colorado, 1978
Associate, business litigation firm, 1978-81
Partner in another business litigation firm, 1981-86
Currently, M.B.A. candidate and part-time management consultant

Michael's Statement: I wanted to be a litigator because it seemed more exciting to switch from thing to thing, case to case, fact situation to fact situation. I couldn't see myself sitting down all the time, grinding away in corporate law.

My first couple years out of law school, I was bored. I didn't like the discovery aspect of trial work; the "sitting-at-my-desk" part. I liked the rare moments I had in court when I'd get a kick of adrenaline from showing my stuff; being articulate under pressure, and occasionally doing the right thing by getting a horrible witness to contradict himself, or seeing someone who deserved it get his due. It was the trial game that was the thrill.

The intellectual aspect of law was a continuing plus. But if anything is overrated, it is how smart you have to be to be a lawyer. The legal system, at least the litigation side of it, is devoted to soft, oily, human questions not easily reducible to intellectual formulas. So you don't have to be a rocket scientist to be a good lawyer. In fact, some of the best litigators aren't smart at all, just more empathetic.

When you practice law, you speak in a special language and deal with people in black robes who are treated like they are God's very emissaries on Earth. There's a kind of vague, religious overtone associated with the entire process; a majesty and formality that you don't have in other professions. It makes you a more serious person for doing it, but it also separates you from the real world.

I left law because I was tired of being on the periphery of life. I could work for somebody in some kind of lawsuit, and the only people who cared about the result were the parties involved. The work was devoid of meaning. When I think about what I was contributing, or even accomplishing, it gets down to something as simple as a transfer of wealth from Car A to Car B in a traffic accident, or from Railroad A to Passenger B in a train mishap, or from Shareholder A to Shareholder B in a business deal. In the end, it didn't make much difference.

I was a lawyer for seven years. After the first two or three, I started thinking about leaving. Practicing law as a litigator in Des Moines, I felt I was in a backwater of a backwater. I was bored silly. I could see myself playing golf on the same course my father did, making a comfortable living in Des Moines as a lawyer. But it didn't excite me. I stayed the next four years only because I couldn't figure a way out. What I want to do now is something that has an effect on the way people live.

THE LAWYER-ENTREPRENEUR

Lawyers rely on precedent to recommend action; their advice always presumes a reasonably certain expectation of the outcome. Lawyers also pick apart and criticize, typically perpetuating a variation of some proven approach, rather than testing a novel alternative. The whole superstructure of the profession is based on avoiding risk. Entrepreneurs, on the other hand, forge new ground by exercising their creativity. In that sense, being a lawyer and being an entrepreneur is almost a contradiction in terms.

To attorneys who find joy in creative problem-solving, or who thrive in an imaginative atmosphere, functioning within the legal system can be a constant frustration. After suffering that frustration for over seven years in the bankruptcy departments of three high-pressure Manhattan firms, *Rees'* creativity now earns him personal fulfillment as well as financial success.

◆

Rees' Profile

B.A., Harvard University, 1973
J.D., Columbia Law School, 1977
Associate at three different law firms, 1977-84
Sales representative, legal software firm, 1984-87
Currently, vice-president, legal software firm

Rees' Statement: The law fits people who are comfortable with hierarchies, and who enjoy focusing intensely and deeply on certain problems. I moved from law school to the bankruptcy department of a huge New York firm because I thought helping businesses get back on their feet would be the most creative area of law. As a low-level associate, though, I wasn't paid to be creative. There were certain things I could and couldn't do; I had to keep to the tried and true forms. It was all so confining. With hindsight, I can see that I didn't fit in.

In business, on the other hand, there's no such structure and I love it. I try to think of what's the best thing to do in the unknown situation. I find that completely challenging. There are no answers. You're scared, and you do what you think is reasonable.

Throughout seven years of practicing law, my insecurity ran rampant. For years, I had a complex that I was a fraud, an imposter, and in just a matter of time, I was going to be discovered. Yes, I was a National Merit Scholar; yes, somehow I got into Harvard; yes, Columbia took me on a scholarship and I clerked for a prestigious firm. But somewhere I had the feeling it was going to catch up with me. At different times, I went to three therapists who all took me in different directions. Nothing helped.

The fear disappeared the minute I stopped practicing law. Funny about that, isn't it?

When I practiced law, I probably spent more hours at the office than I do here. But, because I was unhappy, I would walk out of the door and try to forget about it. Now, I'm much more committed to my work. I go home at night, and after my son goes to bed, I turn on the computer. My work and my play cross over.

Most people look at the law as a lucrative profession. When the median income in the United States is $21,000, a lawyer making $80,000 a year looks really good. But, there are true income limits to being a lawyer. Even the top lawyers, the freaks in a sense, make under a million dollars. In business, if you're successful and go public, as Bill Gates of Microsoft did, you could be 31 years old and a billionaire.

Money is a motivator to me. But I hope I have enough sense to see that pursuing the dollar for its own sake drives you crazy. I make a lot of money in what I'm doing here; I'm not complaining. But more importantly, I like knowing that if I work hard, and if we get some more people to do well, we may go public. Who knows? Maybe at 40 I'll be able to retire. In which case the real question is: what would I do if I retired?

The answer is easy: I'd keep doing this.

THE LAWYER-INTEGRATOR

In 1984, *Barrister* magazine reported that nearly half of all lawyers worked in excess of eight hours per day and could not take enough vacation to relieve the pressure.[2] At that time, the average annual time requirement at large law firms was 1,800 billable hours. In 1988, several New York City firms upped the ante to 2,500 hours per year, which translates to eight hours per day, six days per week, every week of the year. No vacation. No holidays. No sick leave. No Saturdays off.

Added to a lawyer's already full day's work are such tasks as billing, business and social meetings, committee work, training, pro bono and bar association contribution, not to mention the more mundane moments in everyone's work day — conversing with co-workers, helping out a staff member, or just visiting the lavatory. In other words, to satisfy business and professional obligations, and still leave time to eat, sleep, commute, and take care of personal needs, the attorney devotes six entire days out of seven each week to law, with an occasional Sunday to collapse in exhaustion. "The quid pro quo at large law firms is dazzling," says District of Columbia lawyer, former ambassador and international negotiator Sol Linowitz. "We attract them, we lure them, we bribe them, and in the process we don't tell them that they're going to be giving up a decent way of life."[3]

As work hours consume more and more of every day, family and personal needs rank a distant second to the demands of lawyering.[4] "I get the feeling that I am nothing more than a utility, like the lights or the water," admits a practitioner from San Jose, California. "The clients flip my switch and I'm just supposed to turn on. This year, though, I became a father for the first time, and I don't want to be a utility anymore. I want to watch my daughter grow up."

What distinguishes Lawyer-Integrators from other practitioners is that they choose to reject the hectic legal lifestyle for one that is slower-paced, and that integrates work and play, family and career, and home and community. Phillip Moffitt, publisher and editor-in-chief of *Esquire* magazine, described this phenomenon of commercially successful individuals choosing to drop out of the corporate rat race as "cooling out." To Moffitt, the choice represents not only a "jump in the quality of life," but a recommitment "to those ideals and dreams they had at the beginning of their adult lives."[5]

At one time, *Earl* enjoyed the challenge of building up a successful small law practice, developing a good professional reputation, and handling every type of legal matter at least once. Those demands, though, became intolerable after the births of his two children. And since he could not cut down on his work hours to devote more time to his young family, this Lawyer-Integrator said "good-bye" to the law.

◆

Earl's Profile

B.A., Miami University, 1967
M.A., Ohio University, 1968
U.S. Air Force, 1969-73
J.D., Boston University, 1976
Self-employed private practitioner, 1976-84
Currently, ceramics entrepreneur

Earl's Statement: In 1981, I made a list of all the things that were wrong with my life. Lifestyle was what it all boiled down to.

We are only here once. We've only got our kids for X number of years, and then it's all over. What we do as lawyers is frivolous compared to that. Nobody remembers who did *Hadley v. Baxendale* or any other case. We're nobodies. Let's face it! So, if we're never going to make a name that's lasting as a lawyer, or do anything tangible, it all comes down to what kind of life we're going to live. For me, it all boiled down to lying down on a flat log in the sun and enjoying my family.

What bothered me most about practicing law was what I call "kamikaze lawyers." They enter the profession without any life experience and provide services at a price that nobody can compete with. Their businesses quickly go down the tubes because their clients don't pay them. But in the meantime, they engage in economic warfare in which they're willing to commit suicide.

Every time these kamikazes would file a pleading, I had to file something to respond to them to protect my client. My wife and I practiced together and we would set up these elaborate babysitting schedules to hold our lives together. All it took to ruin that schedule — and our lives — was a kamikaze with five days and a typewriter, dragging us into court on some hearing.

I tried very hard to cope within the practice of law. I dumped

35

my trial practice and started something called the Debt Relief Clinic, doing nothing but bankruptcies. The beauty of bankruptcy practice is that it operates under an incredibly fixed schedule. Motions were always Friday morning. The Chapter 7's were on Thursday afternoon. Nobody could pull anything on me. And, more importantly, bankruptcies are fungible. They all look the same; anybody can take them. I got together with a couple of other lawyers so that we could all take each other's files in for the meetings of creditors. Each of us had to go in only once a month. We could plan out our whole year's schedule that way.

It was a much easier way to practice, and easier to handle emotionally. My life was much more relaxed from a scheduling standpoint alone. Things began to fall apart, though, when we had our second child. We could coordinate with one; but the second child added an extra burden that we could not handle.

By then I was getting seriously burned out. I was less and less tolerant of people wasting my time because my time was now my kids' time. It sounds trite, but kids grow up so fast. Those first four or five years are so precious. The thought of any slob taking that time away from me and that child seemed worth killing over.

I found it hard to be civil, and it was coming out in court. Somebody would call a hearing, and if I thought it was stupid I would say the rudest things. I wrote nasty remarks in letters, calling people vile names. I took great pleasure in letting the whole world know if a certain lawyer pissed me off. I was always on the brink of exploding — with the client or the judges or the other attorneys — because this wasn't a game anymore. This was deadly serious and I was eating myself up with bitterness. Sooner or later, I knew it was going to spill out in a way that would get me held in contempt of court.

Then, in 1982, I happened to see some ceramic Christmas tree ornaments that appealed to me. I knew nothing about the technique of making them, but I bought one anyway and went around to ceramics stores and crafts outlets, trying to figure out what glaze was used and how the colors were applied.

After hundreds of false starts, I made a small run of my own Christmas ornaments. They sold pretty well. The following spring, my wife and I entered ourselves in a gift show and got a sales rep. A few months later, I was already spending far more of my time making Christmas ornaments than practicing law. Ceramics became my first priority. I told the secretaries that if I was on the phone talking about selling the ornaments, I didn't care if a Supreme Court Justice called, everything else went on hold. It got to the point where I was working at the law office only as long as the parking meter would last — 120 minutes at a time. I went in and moved through all of my work as fast as I could. I booked clients every quarter hour. The minute it looked like bankruptcy wasn't an appropriate option, I sent them out the door. I wasn't there serving coffee to people.

I cut out every ounce of dead weight. Every minute at the office was productive so I had big blocks of time to devote to the ornaments. By the fall, it looked like the business would fly, and we packed up our office and left.

I have some friends from law school who are making fantastic sums of money but paying for it by living wretched lives. As for me, I'd rather take the good life first and figure out later how to get the money to support it.

Even so, with last year's business, I'm going to pay more in income tax than one third of what most lawyers will ever earn. Economically, I've got no complaints. We go to Hawaii, or the Caribbean, with the kids for spring vacation. In the summer, we sail our 40-foot sailboat two weeks out of every month. I'm also off from about a week before Christmas until mid-January. Our lifestyle has incredibly improved.

THE LAWYER-SUPER WOMAN

Lawyer-Super Women want to succeed equally at mothering and lawyering, but they leave the profession when they realize the futility of their goal.

In the early 1970's, women flooded into law school on the waves of the feminist movement. Since then, their relative numbers in the profession have steadily increased, even in the face of record growth in law school enrollment and in the overall population of practicing

37

lawyers. Four percent of those who entered law school in 1963 were women. A decade later, their representation leaped to 20 percent, and had doubled again by 1986.[6] In 1976, women represented nine percent of all practicing attorneys. Ten years later, their numbers had quadrupled to constitute almost a fifth of the lawyer population.[7]

Today, even though women enter and excel in law school, their competence is not automatically assumed. Most find that they have to prove themselves by bettering their male peers. To do so, they seem to dive into law practice with more energy, commitment, and compulsiveness than most men. Ralph Warner, lawyer-turned-publisher, says he was alarmed by the behavior of the women lawyers he once supervised. "The basic idiocy of the legal system seemed less apparent to them," he observed. "They were naively delighted with it all, and wondering, 'Can I run the meeting and write the brief and then stay up all night to prepare?' From my own sexist perspective, it seemed that wearing a suit, having a briefcase, and being known as an attorney, was a lot more fun for these women than being a housewife. And at some level, it all seemed so wonderful that they didn't recognize the price they were going to pay."

They pay with their personal lives. Today, women lawyers are more than twice as likely as men to be single, and three times as likely to be childless.[8] Those women who do marry and become parents contend with "traditional attitudes that reflect a double-edged sexism; attitudes that say a man must give everything to his career or be considered weak, and that a woman cannot give everything to her career and still be a good wife or mother."[9]

Sharon is one of the Lawyer-Super Women. In the eight years after she graduated from law school, *Sharon* held four different jobs as a lawyer. She tried academia, public interest law, legal publishing, and private practice. Her focus ranged from counseling to administration; from litigation to legal research and writing; from day care regulation to school bond issues. But none of it seemed to complement her roles as wife and mother. Only after sacrificing her marriage and moving into a non-law position was *Sharon* successful in balancing her family and work commitments.

Sharon's Resume

M.A., English literature, 1968
English instructor at the college level, 1968-76
J.D., University of Chicago Law School, 1980
Instructor, legal research and writing, 1981
Public interest lawyer, 1981-84
Associate, corporate law firm, 1984-85
Writer and editor for legal publisher, 1985-87
Currently, law school assistant dean for students

Sharon's Statement: I noticed a huge difference between being a student with three young children and being an attorney with three young children. As a student, I could do what I needed to do fairly easily. As a lawyer, it was very hard. I was always frantic and conflicted, thinking, "I should be home with the children; I should be here at work." Everything had to be so carefully calculated in terms of time and who was responsible when. It seemed that there was a constant crisis or near-crisis all of the time. I was always juggling too many things.

My first job as a practicing attorney — director of a public interest project devoted to children's issues — was originally set up as a 30-hour per week commitment. I was dedicated to a part-time arrangement. But in 1981 the conventional wisdom was that practicing law part-time could not be done if you wanted to have a serious practice. So, after the first year, the board voted to switch my position to full time with a proportionate increase in income. I fought the decision long and hard but eventually lost.

It was not a good trade-off for me. Full-time practice meant spending all day in the city, bringing a lot of work home, attending many night meetings and sometimes working through the weekends. I had to do all of the fund-raising, manage the office, and take care of the clients. It was much more than I could handle given that it didn't pay enough for me to have the amount of child care I really needed. When I look back at what made me leave the children's rights project, it was, ironically, the demands of my own family.

When I am under a lot of stress, I wake up at two in the morning and can't go back to sleep. Back then, I was doing it constantly. At one point, I had a serious bout of pneumonia, which I am sure was 90 percent stress-induced. I got to thinking that there had to be a better way to live.

Fortunately, my husband got a job offer in Denver. It was a difficult decision, but we were both ready for a change. We thought a less high-powered environment would make our marriage work better.

I worked for a midsize Denver firm for a year, slowly working into advising school districts on their elections. We did some corporate work for the hospitals. The firm was generous in paying for the bar, and giving me a month off with salary to study for it.

I thought I had finally achieved a balance among my obligations. But the morning I was to take the bar, my husband told me that he was moving back to Illinois — whether or not I wanted to come — and that he was inviting our teenage kids to return to the Chicago area, and their friends, with him. We did move back, but that episode finished our marriage.

After my husband moved out, I took a job with a legal publisher. I wondered if I would be happier in a job with less stress and excitement, and with regular hours. All I discovered was that working at something too easy and boring has its own stresses. In my present job at the law school, however, I'm still working in a legal environment, but my schedule is manageable and predictable. Fall is very busy and stressful; spring is busy but manageable. The summer, when my children are on vacation, is quiet; a time for me to catch up and reassess what I am doing.

People often ask if I'm ever going to go back into practice. The answer is yes, probably. But not until I feel less of an obligation to be available to my last child at home and very likely, even then, on a volunteer basis only. You see, to be truthful, I do not miss the practice of law at all.

THE LAWYER-PEACEMAKER

Lawyer-Peacemakers strive to bring order out of chaos with artful diplomacy. They work hard to create an atmosphere in which enemies lay down their swords and sign meaningful treaties. To do so, they help their clients concentrate on common interests rather than emphasizing differences. In other words, this category of lawyers is oriented to "win/win"[10] solutions, considering "settlement" synonymous with "conflict resolution." But, since "win/lose"[11] is still the foundation of the adversarial system, Lawyer-Peacemakers are constantly at loggerheads with the majority of lawyers who consider negotiation only as a means to get more for their clients and less for the other side. In the end, the Lawyer-Peacemakers acknowledge the futility of pursuing their mission in the adversarial system.

If it seemed a realistic way to earn a living, some Lawyer-Peacemakers might remain in the profession as mediators (referees who guide opposing parties toward a self-created solution). Until very recently, though, lack of public awareness of the mediation alternative, combined with the legal profession's skepticism about the process, resulted in limited opportunities for earnings. Most bar association sponsored programs, in fact, are still staffed by volunteers who contribute their time solely to reduce the backlog of cases pending in the courts. Lately, however, corporate demand for less costly and more rapid resolution of disputes has supported the growth of such companies as United States Arbitration & Mediation, Judicial Arbitration & Mediation Services, Inc., and Endispute, Inc., all owned and operated by lawyers. But, the general public still seems less willing to pay one person to help them work things out, than to pay two different people to blame the other side or avoid responsibility. And, unfortunately, now that the legal establishment is becoming involved with mediation, the same strictly orchestrated formality that has left the adversarial system so unwieldy is being interjected into the process.

In August, 1986, *Linda* was a business-suited, bow-tied deputy prosecutor who directed officers of the court, negotiated with attorneys, planned, analyzed, promoted, demoted and fired. A year later, after failing to find a reasonable alternative for her inclinations as a Lawyer-Peacemaker, *Linda* created a niche that was much more personally rewarding. Now, she bales hay, grooms pack animals and plans menus for her guided gourmet camping trip business in the Pacific Northwest.

Linda's Profile

B.A., Marshall University, 1973
M.A., clinical psychology, Marshall University, 1974
Police department counselor, 1974-76
J.D., University of Puget Sound Law School, 1979
Deputy prosecuting attorney, 1979-86
Currently, part-time counselor and operator of North Cascades Llama
    Company

Linda's Statement: At one time, I would have said lawyers were
really good people who simply had a job to do. But now, after a
number of years watching other attorneys practice, I've decided
otherwise. I know some lawyers enter the profession to bring about
justice, and to make the system better. But I saw plenty of other
lawyers come into the prosecutor's office merely as a fast track into a
civil litigation firm where they could make a lot of money. Those
were the lawyers who tried to win, win, win all of their cases, even
if it wasn't just or fair. Because, if they won, the firms figured they
were smarter, faster, and more predatory, and they got hired.

I was definitely one of those lawyers who went into law in order
to seek justice. I felt very strongly about my work as a prosecutor of
sexual offenders. I loved dealing with victims, and being the good
guy. When I knew I was doing the absolutely right thing, I felt great.

But, the inter-family abuse cases were especially hard. Often
what was required by statute wasn't the best solution. And when I
put a kid on the witness stand to testify against a father or brother or
uncle, a big part of me screamed, "This isn't helping the family; it's
tearing it apart." I agonized a lot over those cases. I sent a lot of kids
from dysfunctional families to institutions that had no resources to
help them, and just spewed them back out onto the street with the
same basic problems. It was one great big circle. After a while, I felt
like shouting, "Nobody is solving anybody's problems. Nobody is
helping anything."

As long as I live, I'll never forget sitting in a juvenile courtroom,
listening to a public defender make ludicrous objections to everything. Each time she was overruled, she elbowed her 16-year-old

client and laughed to him, "Well, it was worth a try." In effect, she was telling this kid that it was all a big game and he was playing it too.

That's what the adversarial system is: a place where you put on your gloves and duke it out in court; a place where you can be awful and obnoxious to each other, and then take your gloves off to be best buddies again. Well, I just can't live that way. Law is not a good profession for a person who is accustomed to dealing with other individuals rationally, reasonably and in a framework where people actually have a meeting of the mind. Law is not a negotiating field; it is an adversarial field.

There ought to be a required stage of the legal process where the parties sit down at a table before they even get into court. They would try to reach a solution in a give-and-take atmosphere. But in order to do that, lawyers would have to get down to the concrete issues; they'd have to act as advisers and counselors rather than advocates. If mediation were made mandatory in every case, creating an atmosphere in which the wholly adversarial lawyer would be out of place and uncomfortable, a lot of people — lawyers and clients — would go away with solutions, and retain a better feeling about the whole process.

Even with that procedure imposed on litigants, though, there would still be the lawyer who advises his client in a marriage dissolution action, "Skip that mediation garbage. Let's go to court and fight." There will always be the option to go right into duking it out. Unfortunately, there isn't anything I can do to change that. Besides, my experience up here in the mountains — grooming and training the llamas and developing this business — is too much fun to want to look back.

THE LAWYER-ALTRUIST

Lawyer-Altruists expect to practice law graciously, in just the same way they remember Gregory Peck playing Atticus Finch in the film version of *To Kill a Mockingbird*. They want to uplift the downtrodden, be an advocate for the oppressed, and bring peace to the lives of those in great turmoil, confusion and pain.

Lawyer-Altruists are neither unusual nor delusional. In one American Bar Association study, the pursuit of justice on behalf of the disadvantaged or powerless was the most frequently stated reason for choosing to go to law school.[12] Lawyers have made news headlines by advocating the rights of welfare recipients and the disabled, and by seeking to clarify rights protected by the Constitution. Without a doubt, criminal law attorneys are motivated by the desire to see justice done — as prosecutors, by trying to protect society; as defense lawyers, by assuring that the accused receive the law's due process. Other practitioners help families deal sensibly and kindly with their losses, whether from death, injury, disagreement, or divorce.

The satisfaction of being a helper diminishes, however, as the Lawyer-Altruist realizes that the adversarial system often does as much bad as it does good. As a "hired gun" who uses logic and posturing to resolve emotionally-based disputes, Lawyer-Altruists come to realize that their representation often ends up aggravating their clients' situations more than it resolves them. First of all, their advocacy highlights disagreement and heightens emotions by drawing boundaries between the sides. Then, they place their clients' controversies at the mercy of an inefficient and unpredictable court system which might put off resolution of the lawsuit for five or six years. What is most dismaying, however, is how Lawyer-Altruists inhibit their clients' healing process. By seeking compensation for their clients' "pain and suffering," Lawyer-Altruists unintentionally encourage them to regard themselves as helpless victims for as long as their case remains pending (a professor at Yale has even documented and named this ailment, "jurisgenic disease"). Eventually, Lawyer-Altruists conclude that the adversarial system — and their roles as advocates — impedes the closure of their clients' conflicts.

Kate applied to law school in order to do something important and secure. After practicing for eight years, however, she had enough experience to understand that she could not do enough good to combat the all too often wasteful and unfair actions of her opponents. *Kate* dropped out of the legal system when she could no longer continue to participate with passion and conviction.

Kate's Profile

B.A., Miami University, 1967
M.A., Ohio University, 1968
High school teacher, 1969-1973
J.D., Boston University, 1976
Self-employed private practitioner, 1976-84
Currently, part-time bookkeeper and marketing director for home-
based ceramics business (see Earl's Lawyer-Integrator profile)

Kate's Statement: Before I got into the profession, I had the same general perception of lawyers as the lay public. Law was a serious business, a career you did for life. To me, law was a noble calling, and getting sworn into the bar was the proudest day of my life.

I went into the practice of law with my whole heart. I lived law. I was in court every single day, and I loved the excitement of it. It was like the smell of greasepaint to an actress. I ate lunch every day with the people I met in court that morning. It was fun to belong to, and share an interest with, such a broad group of people. To have practiced law was for me, as a female, a pinnacle. After a while though, it was like being at the circus and hitting the gong. Once I hit that bell, I didn't need to pick up the mallet again. And the longer I practiced, the more frustrated I became by problems inherent in the adversarial system.

First of all, it seems lawyers have to do bad things to do a good job. On top of that, they're always having to excuse the system to their clients. Outrageous things happen; and lawyers have to defend them as if they created the system, while the whole time they're equally sick about what's happened. And the system accomplishes so little. At most, it keeps people from shooting each other. At most. Sometimes, it causes them to.

Practicing law wasn't problem resolution; it was problem-causing. Too often I saw lawyers do the wrong thing. Instead of helping people through the legal process, they blew things into a big, emotionally wrenching issue. They weren't helping. They were hired guns.

I began to wonder why lawyers weren't getting together and saying, "It's true we're adversarial to the point of protecting our clients' interests, but we're two adults. How can we help them?" I began to feel that I was the only one who thought a conscientious attorney had a duty to call the other side and say, "Can we help these people? Can we do what's neat and quick to shield them from bitterness?"

I believe that lawyers are people who were given more — more sense, more brains — than other people. And, I believe they have a duty to use this extra sense to help others in our society who didn't get as much. Lawyers should be more than just technicians, more than tools of their clients. They should be bigger than the people they're serving. They should have wisdom, and some human under-standing, and use their knowledge and smarts to help people.

But so many lawyers don't seem to feel they have a duty to tell the client that he's wrong. They don't tell the man who comes in on a personal injury matter, "Well shoot! This little scar on your knee isn't going to hurt you. Take your lumps. Pick yourself up and walk." They don't tell the couple who want to go bankrupt that they shouldn't file for bankruptcy. If those same clients went to a doctor and said, "I want my appendix taken out" — and that doctor took out their appendix on their say-so — those same lawyers could sue the doctor for letting the patient diagnose himself. But lawyers aren't that way. You go in diagnosing that you need a bankruptcy. They say, "Sure, $500 and it's yours."

I don't know where character comes from. It isn't taught when you're 25. You don't learn it out of a book. So much of this comes from experience. Lawyers have to develop it themselves. But it's too big of a problem among lawyers to become a crusader against it. I'm *not* Mother Teresa.

I lost hope as a lawyer. Life lost its sparkle. As Earl and I were closing our practice, we bought a sailboat and named it "New Hope." That's how I felt about quitting law. That by doing so, my magic would come back, like the month of March when the sap starts running again.

THE LAWYER-HUMANIST

Lawyer-Humanists resent the situational morality they are required as advocates to adopt. Because they are taught in law school that only a poor attorney chooses sides, they represent individuals with stands that offend their own values. Or they find themselves arguing a position for one client that is the exact opposite of what they must argue for the next. Eventually, some may end up feeling like prostitutes who, for a price, according to one former practitioner, will argue "indefensible positions for people in untenable situations."[13]

Lawyer-Humanists might accept this conflict if they believed their advocacy was ultimately of great benefit to society, or to those they represent. Instead, they know that truth and justice seldom emerge out of the adversarial system, and that battles are often won by attrition, by deep pockets, by caginess, and sometimes, sadly, by cheating.

Norm entered law school because of his interest in assuring that citizens be treated justly. It wasn't long before he discovered that the adversarial system does not reward lawyers for achieving justice; it rewards them for winning. Once he understood that, as a hired gun, he was seeking to "forcibly extract money from one party to give to another," and that the system encouraged him to accomplish that task by "creating confusion," *Norm* began his journey out of the legal profession.

◆

Norm's Profile

B.A., University of Texas, 1965
Vice-president and general manager, swimming pool equipment
        company, 1966-71
J.D., University of Texas, 1971
Solo practitioner and associate, small general law practice, 1971-76
Law clerk to solo practitioner, 1976-78
M.S.W., University of Texas, 1978
Social worker, 1978-80
Manager, Juvenile Court diversion program, 1980-83
Director, Juvenile Court operations and volunteer programs, 1983-87
Currently, seminar leader and consultant

Norm's Statement: I can remember only once in my life when I had what I thought was a migraine headache. A partner had assigned me a personal injury case that was coming up for trial. Even though no good witnesses had been found for our clients, I was told I had to try it. On the day I had to take the deposition of a treating doctor, I was driving down the freeway, and I actually lost part of my peripheral vision. It scared the hell out of me. That was followed by an intense headache that lasted for three days, and didn't respond to either barbiturates or any other powerful pain medication. I know now that my body was only responding to the conflict I experienced practicing law.

In law school, I focused on being the super-rational, super-intellectual super-logician. I submitted to a lobotomy of my emotional corpus. I had to eliminate all that emotional experience stuff to get down to the computer-like mind. I tried to do it as a lawyer, too, and I was unhappy. Because even though there is a large part of me that is logical and rational, it's not natural for me to be that way all the time.

I was a fairly good trial lawyer, but I hated it. Absolutely hated it. I don't thrive on combat or on conflict. I'm not a Type A competitive personality. And I often felt that my client didn't have much more right to win, or to the money, than the person we were suing. Often, I would ask myself why I didn't shake my client and say, "Look you idiot, why don't you settle this thing? This is ridiculous. Do you realize the amount of work we're going to be doing and the chance of getting what we want? You were partly at fault anyway."

Instead, if it was legally reasonable and not illegal or unethical, I would support my client's position as far as possible. I felt that it was my obligation as an advocate to do so. The way I did it was to convince myself that my client's position was "the" right and fair one to reach. But it was all just a whole lot of intellectual masturbation; a game I played in order to stay in the role and not hate myself. Because, you know, fairness is always in the eye of each individual. People tend to see justice from their own limited perspective. It totally differs from person to person, and it certainly differs between the two people in a lawsuit. That's why they are in the courtroom. They have already been through the screening process of fairness or they wouldn't have ended up in court.

I've always been interested in justice and in treating people in a just way. But it seems that many lawyers are not interested in justice; they're interested in winning. That's the nature of the beast. All lawyers want to win, and sometimes way beyond wanting justice; not only because they'll be rewarded with money if they win, but because their ego is involved. It comes down to, "Am I the fastest gun?" Their egos and their reputations are on the line. Most people don't understand that. They worry that their lawyer is not going to do a good job for them. I tell them, "Listen, that lawyer is going to sweat blood for you. He is going to do more for you than you can imagine, way more than you are going to pay for. But he is going to do it because of his own ego, not because of you."

And sometimes a lawyer wants to win so badly that he does marginally unethical things. Sandbagging. Ambushing the other side at trial by coming up with hidden agendas or hidden witnesses. Even getting witnesses to say things that aren't true. I ran into that fairly early on while trying cases. Amazing things, too, like faking photographs, records disappearing when I'd subpoena them, or other things that weren't entirely illegal but changed the way the evidence looked to the jury. That was what some lawyers did who badly wanted to win. I saw it all the time. That's one of the big flaws in the adversarial system; that lawyers are so totally bent on winning.

Although I found myself pretty heavily caught up in winning, I also had a strong moral streak. I didn't lose my own sense of values or I wouldn't have felt the tension. But I did feel a lot of pressure to compromise and to set my values aside. The way I see it, when you wrestle with a pig, you're going to get covered with mud.

About the same time I decided to quit practicing law, I was offered a partnership interest which would have meant a threefold increase in my income. I declined, though, because I didn't want to pay the price that came with the money. To me, there were not enough funds available to buy the medicine to handle the pain of living that kind of life.

THE LAWYER-CRUSADER

Entering the profession to save the world, the Lawyer-Crusaders inevitably slam up against the wall of a ponderous and reactionary system.

Those Lawyer-Crusaders who poured into law school in the late 1960's and early 1970's were not disappointed in the early years. The Vietnam War, especially the invasion into Cambodia, was stopped by the power of the law. Schools were integrated. Draft resisters found safe haven. Abortion became legal. Nixon was ousted from office. It seemed that all the wrongs of society could be righted by working within the legal system. And all one had to do to wield that power was go to law school and pass the bar.

But those power trips were short-lived. After struggling to restore government benefits to unfairly deprived citizens, the Lawyer-Crusaders realized that they were merely shifting money from one recipient to another without any more money overall being targeted to the disadvantaged. More significantly, poverty lawyers were crippled as effective advocates when the government created the Legal Services Corporation, severely restricting their use of the class action lawsuit as a tool to represent huge numbers of otherwise powerless people, and their intervention in controversial areas such as abortion rights and school desegregation. With Reagan in office, federal funding for legal assistance to the poor slowed to a trickle, and was regularly threatened with complete termination.

Ralph Warner was a self-described "quintessential hippie lawyer" who went to law school to change the world. When he became disillusioned with the law's real ability to change anything, he dropped out of lawyering without sacrificing his notion of making a significant contribution to society. What began as his service to the poor has now evolved into a financially successful legal self-help publishing business, a venture much more compatible with his spiritual proclivities than battling in court to move dollars from one pocket to another.

Ralph Warner's Profile

B.A., Princeton University, 1963
J.D., Boalt Hall, University of California, 1966
Clerk, 9th Circuit Court of Appeals, 1966-67
Legal aid and legal clinic lawyer, 1967-71
Author, The Independent Paralegal's Handbook, 1986; 29 Reasons
  Not to Go to Law School, 1987; Everybody's Guide to Small
  Claims Court, 1988; and numerous other self-help law books[14]
Currently, co-owner and publisher of Nolo Press

Warner's Statement: I went into law because I somehow saw it as a way to make money while, at the same time, doing good. Since then, though, I've learned that life doesn't compensate poets well.

After graduation, I ran out and did what a whole lot of other people did: I joined Legal Aid and immediately filed a bunch of court actions against all of these huge and gross unfairnesses. When I went into Legal Aid, my father was horrified. About a year later, he was sending me articles from the *Wall Street Journal* saying 99 of the 106 brightest law students in the country turned their backs on law firms to go into poverty law. Nobody was on law review anywhere without wanting to go into some kind of public interest work. You could go into Legal Aid and be walking into federal court tomorrow suing anybody you wanted. It was the greatest thing going. At age 25, 26, 27, I was on the front page of the newspapers every day. For a couple years out of law school, I was power-tripping on the whole thing.

We were able to shift some money from here to there; to win some individual cases. Anyone who was in Legal Aid during that time was proud of it. But I saw so many of these cases as merely winning $30 million here and moving it there without any more money being spent on the poor. The federal courts didn't make the poor less poor. They just took money away from somebody else so the game could go on forever. It got to the point that I couldn't write another grant, or go before another unresponsive legislative committee, or file another court action that was going to be buried.

After five years, most of the people who went into law for altruistic reasons — myself included — were burned out and unhappy. I looked very hard for another way to live because it seemed that law didn't work. It produced a certain amount of money, but it didn't produce any poetry. And I really wanted to do something to change things for the better. Why? Because I was one of the people for whom the whole American dream worked: I grew up in the suburbs, passed all the SATs with flying colors, went to exactly the right schools, and got all the right degrees. But by the time I was 25 years old, I felt like I had done it all. And at age 28, I quit everything.

Ed Sherman, my former partner here at Nolo Press, worked with me at Contra Costa Legal Services and quit about nine months before I did. Between the two of us we had five kids, and neither he nor I knew what to do next. So, we ran a legal clinic out of the backyard. While running this clinic, Ed and I realized that half of the employees at Legal Aid only existed to tell people they weren't poor and miserable enough to qualify for free legal services. And yet those people had no other place to go. At some point, Ed wrote instructions to do your own divorce, put some staples in the side of it and ran it off as a quasi-book. It sold 500 copies.

Fortunately, the bar association attacked it as dangerous without ever having read it. What luck! Suddenly we were selling a couple thousand copies a month. Since then, we've sold over 450,000 copies of the divorce book in California, and now 35 percent of the population handles their own divorces.

I don't have a grand plan in running this business, but I do have my own personal plan. I don't want to commute. I don't want to work 90 hours a week. I don't want to be too greedy. I want to continue to have fun, like writing my book, *29 Reasons Not to Go to Law School* . What appeals to me is the notion of empowering people with the tools to represent themselves. It satisfies a part of me that needs to be on the right side of the world.

I don't know that anybody is ever going to change the world's view about sharing everything. We are basically pretty greedy monkeys and the world's always been a pretty unfair place. But to the extent that anybody changes anything, they get there by walking step by step from where they are to where they want to be.

Talking about it, arguing in court, filing papers doesn't change it. Doing it changes it. In that sense, I hope that my experience with Nolo serves as a model for others.

THE LAWYER-VISIONARY

Lawyer-Visionaries react to the adversarial system with their own notion of a world that works peacefully. One former practitioner described the conflict this way: "Law is push/pull, win/lose, constantly adversarial. It deals with easements and off-shore leases; with pushing papers back and forth. Law is not a vehicle for transformation. It is the lubricant that allows society to handle its conflicts and run its businesses."

Lawyer-Visionaries start out with a commitment to bring clients and their opponents together. To do so, they ignore the baiting of hostile opposing counsel and keep their eyes focused on a peaceful conclusion. Sooner or later, though, they adopt some of the demeanor of their opponents: a little less patient, a little more aggressive and riveted to their position, a little less willing to see the other side as anything but unreasonable and overreaching. When Lawyer-Visionaries take full stock of their slide into disagreeable conformance, they leave the profession for a more receptive and supportive environment.

Arnold Patent, who commented on the nature of the adversarial system in the last chapter, withdrew from the practice of law after accepting that his adversarial and competitive orientation to life was producing the constant physical pain he experienced. In the process of meditating to reduce stress, Patent became sensitive to what he calls the "basic laws of the universe." Eventually, he was asked to teach those ideas to others. Nowadays, as author and publisher of two books, Patent leads weekend seminars across the country and networks with others who share his view of the world.

◆

Arnold Patent's Profile

J.D., New York University Law School, 1953
U.S. Army, 1953-55
Solo practitioner, 1955-80
Real estate developer, 1978-80
Author, You Can Have It All, 1984, and Death Taxes & Other Illusions, 1989
Currently, nationwide seminar facilitator

Patent's Statement: Each of the professions in our society represents a model according to which people practice and live. Lawyers are the model for lawfulness; the basic rules of conduct between people. We are raised to believe that society must be conflict-ridden and that people cannot work out disputes between themselves. Therefore, the traditional model for law is adversarial.

In addition, the underlying belief of all the major professions — medical, legal, accounting, engineering, educational — is that the people who come to the professionals are not as capable as the professional, and therefore cannot handle their own experiences in that particular area without help. We are raised to believe that doctors and lawyers know things about personal health and conflict that other people can't possibly know. The professionals then encourage and solidify that belief by handling everything.

The professionals, though, are only practicing in the way that society wishes them to. Since the adversarial system reflects the current consciousness of society-at-large, lawyers conform to that consciousness. If mediation-minded lawyers took control of the American Bar Association, and voted through changes that made the legal system totally nonadversarial, it still would have no effect. Those people who wanted to beat up on each other, who wanted lawyers to be gladiators, would find them.

The underlying theory of our capitalistic system is that if we have everybody out chasing dollar bills, it will all work itself out; that greed will make our society successful. That's it pure and simple. We sugarcoat it. We try to wrap it up in different packages. But, if we are honest, we have to admit that greed is the major motivating factor.

My perception of the ideal professional is a person who puts himself out of business by helping a client recognize that he or she is totally capable of handling life's situations by him or herself. A lawyer will not be a true professional if his major motivating factor is making money. The two goals are in gross conflict.

The majority of our society still believes that it is better to have money in the bank than to have support from others. But think about it. If you have $100 million in the bank and have a heart attack while surrounded by your six heirs — all of whom despise you — how much good will it do you to offer one of them $1 million to take you to the hospital? On the other hand, if Mother Teresa needs a ride to the hospital but has no money, she's likely to have hundreds of offers. Which is worth more? When people find that supporting other people works better than competing with them, and trying to outsmart or be better than or get more from them, the legal system as we know it will become a matter for historians.

But, don't misunderstand me. The adversarial system won't be terminated by some sort of mandate. It simply will no longer be used, like the horse and buggy. When the automobile came around, people stopped using the horse for major transportation. Nobody said, "Bad horses. Bad horses. We're going to outlaw horses." People just stopped using them as a basic mode of transportation. Then when the bus came in, it became more efficient in certain ways than the automobile. Then came the airplane. And now we're preparing to ride in rocket ships.

Up Against the Wall

He is not only idle who does nothing,
but he is idle who might be better employed.

♦

SOCRATES

As startling as it may sound, more than four attorneys out of every 10 have expressed a desire to work at something other than law.[1] Strangely though, only about eight percent are actively doing something about it.[2] And, even fewer ever break away. "For every attorney who takes the plunge, there are 10 others who wish they had the guts," says one Midwest practitioner.

The whole long process of becoming a lawyer — from the initial applications to law school to the very first returns on their educational investment — creates powerful, long-lasting ties to the legal profession. In the words of restaurateur Andrea Lachman, who left corporate practice four years ago, "A centrifugal force pushes against those who want to leave, pressuring them to stay within the circle."

The pressure develops at the very beginning of their legal careers. Many students apply to this graduate school with no intention of ever practicing law. Then, while they may instantly dislike the curriculum, they feel pressure to finish what they've begun. Later, even though their summer legal internships are uninspiring, they remain attentive to professors and others who admonish them that to skip the actual practice of law would be a waste of education. Once in the practice, those same students often delude themselves into believing that practicing law was a terrific choice. They tell themselves that their discomfort stems from the fact that they're not yet fully competent, or because good cases only come with experience, or because they aren't yet practicing

57

in the right area of law, or with the right colleagues. Year after year, they expect things to get better, perpetuating a never-ending pattern of postponed gratification that clutches them more tightly than ever to their professional identities.

THE BRAINWASHING

1988 was a boom year in applications for law school. According to the Associated Press, the nation's 175 accredited law schools were flooded with more than 300,000 applications from 75,000 students, an 18 percent increase over 1987. It was the largest pool of applicants since 1980 (and a reversal of seven years of declining enrollments).[3] The reason for this renewed interest in law school? College graduates quite candidly declared they wanted to make a lot of money while helping others, and that a law degree seemed the surest ticket.

That justification has been surfacing for a long time. In fact, many current practitioners would probably admit that they followed that same path into the profession: wanting to "do well" while doing some good. In a law school education, they saw a safe, benign, and potentially valuable haven for someone who didn't know what to do next in life. And, a juris doctorate degree looked like the perfect general background for a variety of interesting careers — exactly the kind of educational credential any well-educated, well-rounded, well-respected person would be proud to earn.

Carol Kanarek, past chairperson of the American Bar Association's Young Lawyers Division Career Issues Committee, and a former practicing lawyer herself, complains about "starry-eyed liberal arts graduates" who walk into law school without the faintest idea what lawyers do and how they do it. Larry Richard of LAWGISTICS contends that the legal profession has become "the great repository" of middle and upper-middle class liberal arts graduates. "Most of my clients decided to become lawyers by default," says Richard. "After they eliminated all the other prestigious, professional, white-collar possibilities — either they didn't like the sight of blood, or they thought accounting was boring — law was what was left."

What these applicants do not understand, however, is that law school is not intended for the generalist. It is, instead, an indoctrination into a new way of thinking that significantly alters one's view and approach to the world. Lawyers who leave the profession have described their education as a type of cult experience in which "legal clones" are molded through intimidation, overwork, competition and peer pressure.

The brainwashing begins immediately, when first-year students are compelled to read 19th century British judicial opinions whose Victorian sentence structure and curious logic make for a horror of comprehension. Students find themselves wading through tomes of these case decisions as if interpreting a foreign language, hoping the teacher will flip a switch of enlightenment instead of continuing to feed their confusion.

Months later, the mystery of the casebooks begins to unravel, making the task of absorbing their contents as arduous as studying the *Encyclopedia Brittanica* but not as impossible as deciphering the Dead Sea scrolls. At this point, law students have shifted from stream-of-conscious thought to the beginnings of jurisprudent analysis. The shift occurs in two ways. Since legal analysis rests on precedent, the students are first drilled to apply what has been decided in the past to current conflicts. Students learn to respect tradition, and to forge new ground only if it connects logically with the old.

Gradually, they absorb the second necessary ingredient: a logic based on semantics; a process of picking apart the meaning of words and studying the possible interpretations of a sentence from two or more opposing points of view. In this way, legal analysis is never clouded by feelings. Once the left-brained logic of law is thoroughly assimilated, and emotions appropriately repressed, a corollary emerges. Although answers eventually must be rendered in black and white, students "get it" if they don't get it. The point of it all is to learn to question and complicate rather than to simplify and resolve. By graduation, a diverse group of bright, creative undergraduates has been fashioned into a herd of conventional legal minds.

In response to law school's rigid environment, some drop out in defiance, or compel the school to flunk them out. Others rebel by attending only enough classes to earn passing grades or by abrasively challenging all conventional mores espoused by a professor. Many swallow their medicine without complaint. But most, *David* among them, choose to conform after a tortuous period of adjustment.

♦

David's Profile

B.A., University of Michigan, 1973
M.B.A., University of Colorado, 1974
J.D., Northwestern University School of Law, 1978
Assistant attorney general, 1978-79
Associate, small general practice firm, 1979-83
Solo practitioner, 1983-86
Assistant director, university department of technology transfer,
*   1986-88*
Currently, co-founder of investment banking firm

David's Statement: Law school, at least for the first year or so, was a process of doing something for someone else. I went because I came from a family of professionals; my father was a surgeon, my mother was a professor, and each of my brothers had high-prestige careers in their own right. If I'd had other role models, I probably would have ended up as a Cordon Bleu chef.

Even though I was raised to believe I was precocious, it took me a long time to figure out which end was up in law school. I didn't get the hang of it until late in the game. The secret — and I think most law school graduates would agree — is not so much to think, but to master certain techniques for logic manipulation by enduring a blunt means of torture. It's a sarcastic, sometimes sadistic, means of intimidating students called the "Socratic method."

In its unadulterated application, the Socratic method is a means to direct and develop a student's thought process so that he reaches conclusions from his own effort. But I have only sat in one or two classes in any law school — and that includes Harvard, Berkeley, Michigan, Denver University, and others — where I saw anyone use the Socratic method. What most law professors think of as the

Socratic method consists of asking leading questions and cornering students so that they are forced to come up with conclusions the professor wants, or to sit there looking foolish if they don't. Other than building resentment, I don't know that it teaches much.

In order to avoid being the brunt of intimidation and humiliation, I was not well known for coming to class. But in my final year at law school, I did manage at some point to show up for a criminal procedure course. That day, a friend of mine who was sitting behind me suddenly stood up and said, "Professor, I just thought you'd want to know that the person sitting in front of me is enrolled in your course. You may not have made his acquaintance yet so let me introduce you."

The professor was up at the lecturn, tilting his head in disbelief, trying to figure out how he had lost control.

My (now former) friend continued, "Professor, meet David. David, meet the professor."

I looked up at Fred and down at my criminal procedure book, then looked up at Fred again, picked up the book and heaved it at him.

At that, the professor got off a pretty good example of what passes for the Socratic method. "Well David," the professor said, "I'm glad to see you are, at least, getting some use of your text this semester." Then began the torture, as I stood for another 20 minutes while the professor grilled me about the cases.

Law school and all the steps that one takes afterwards are a process of conformity. It is extremely difficult for graduates to break away from their professional training and not practice law — especially to do something that is completely creative and has no rules or boundaries — coming as they do from that background.

LOCKSTEP INTO THE FIRMS

Fifty years ago, many law graduates heading into practice chose to hang out their own shingles. Today, the pack mentality prevails. According to one study, the percentage of students who enter private law firms upon graduation increased by 50 percent over a 15-year period; from only half of the class of 1969 to nearly three-quarters of the 1981 class.[4]

Skyrocketing law school tuitions are partly to blame. Lower paid public interest positions become financially infeasible for students carrying $20,000 or more in student loans. Even though some schools have instituted "loan forgiveness" programs which partially cancel those debts for each year a graduate works in the public interest, the substantial difference in compensation — as low as a third of that paid to associates in private practice[5] — is hard to justify. Even more disappointing, students who do resist the pressure to pursue attractive salaries are frustrated by the dearth of public service opportunities that await them.

Laurie Albright, Stanford Law School's Director of Career Services, says she is amazed how a legal education takes "an incredibly diverse group of students and shrinks down their interests." Students, she says, believe that they have somehow failed if they don't at least give private practice a try after graduation. Albright cites the following as typical. "Recently, a woman I had been counseling about public interest or non-law career options came in to tell me she'd accepted a job at a big firm. She said, 'I know I'm not going to be happy there. But I'm going to put in my three years, be a better person for it, and then be able to go anywhere I want to next.'

"That's the attitude," concludes Albright. "Get in, get your credentials, establish yourself and then you have options for the rest of your life."

In faded jeans, with shiny, brown hair hanging long and straight, *Elizabeth* seems the typical English grad student. It is easy to believe her when she says she earned a law degree without any clear idea of how to make use of the credential. Now, with the benefit of hindsight, *Elizabeth* admits that she even chose to be a litigator as a response to the peer pressure and the peculiarities of the law school environment. As a result, she began to fantasize about ending her legal career before she even began.

Elizabeth's Profile

B.A., University of Vermont, 1977
J.D., Georgetown University, 1980
Assistant U.S. attorney, 1980-86
Author, published fiction, 1987
Currently, fiction writer and part-time college English teacher

Elizabeth's Statement: I had no vision of what I'd do after I was graduated from law school. In fact, I went to law school as a substitute for getting a Ph.D. in English; three more years of the kind of demanding education that I thought would open a lot of doors. I was really surprised when I started to consider working for a law firm or as a trial lawyer.

To a large extent, my choices were shaped by the opinions of others. I wasn't making decisions based on what I really wanted to do, but on what was held in high esteem. I didn't think of myself as a trial lawyer. Yet, since trial law was what everybody else wanted to do, I went along and said, "Well, yes. I want to do litigation." When the Justice Department offer came along, I listened to everybody's reaction of, "Oh, wow! You got a job with the Justice Department." I said to myself, "Oh! Okay. I guess that's what I ought to want to do."

And, it did seem like the right thing to do. Law school socialized me into a different frame of mind. By the time I got out, it was very natural for me to be going to work as a trial lawyer, even though I was a creative writer at heart.

I knew, even before I started, that I wasn't going to want to spend the rest of my life practicing law. And I never had it as my goal to be a good lawyer. I just wanted to have done it; to have succeeded at it; and then, to be able to walk away from it all.

FOLLOWING ALL THE RULES

Like *Elizabeth*, most law students spend much of their early education trying to jump all the right hurdles. They strive for straight A's and for outstanding SAT scores; for summa cum laude and Phi Beta

63

Kappa; and for editor of law review and Order of the Coif. Inevitably, they buy into the prevailing attitude that practicing law is a post-graduate necessity, and are lured by most accredited law schools into frantic competitions for summer clerk and associate positions.

These are "the country's smartest young people who didn't want to be doctors but knew they wanted to be something," says Steven Brill of *American Lawyer*.[6] After meeting with prospective employers at school, they fly across the country for in-depth interviews, and are wined and dined and treated like royalty. Large law firms spend up to $1 million per year in out-of-pocket expenses (not including attorney time) for this recruitment process, justifying the expense as a necessary cost of doing business.[7] Their purpose in recruiting summer clerks is not to reduce the work load or to make money on them but to entice them to accept an offer to become an associate. "It's very much a seduction process," says William McGeary, director of career planning and placement at the UCLA School of Law.[8]

And seductive it is, for the crème-de-la-crème of law students. They receive lavish treatment throughout the summer. Some firms house them in the best areas of town, pay them up to $1,000 per week and hand them the most interesting legal issues to research. Often, they are taken along to depositions and to court appearances to get a "flavor" of lawyering, and are feted and entertained as well, as a way of demonstrating the stimulating and challenging nature of the work that will supposedly characterize their careers as new associates. In truth, the summer clerking experience blatantly misrepresents the life of a young associate at any major law firm. Recruitment partners deny that their tactics are a white-collar bait-and-switch, insisting that these legal ingenues "know it is not really like that."[9] But the disillusionment expressed by so many of these young associates belies the recruiters' glib assumptions.

The entire recruitment process, including the law schools' "practice or perish" mentality and the priority given to on-campus interviews, transforms aimless students — who chose law school in order to have more time to figure out what to do with the rest of their lives — into "aimless associates."[10] "I was on automatic pilot," says an honors graduate of Rutgers University Law School. "I never had to formulate a life plan." It's no wonder that so many young lawyers end up, a few years down the road, wondering, "How did I get into this mess?"

Cindy sought a law degree to enhance her business skills. She never intended to practice law. But like most of her classmates, she succumbed to law school's competitive spirit, followed all the rules, moved directly into a high-powered corporate law firm, and was disappointed soon after she arrived.

◆

Cindy's Profile

B.A., Dartmouth University, 1974
Sales manager in insurance company, 1974-78
M.B.A., University of Nevada, 1978
J.D., University of California at Davis Law School, 1981
Associate, large corporate law firm, 1981-85
Currently, public affairs producer for a major television network
affiliate

Cindy's Statement: Law school is designed to push all the buttons of overachievers. You never get to a point where you feel you are doing well enough. If you get good grades, then you're supposed to get good interviews, which are supposed to lead to a good job. The competition never ends. I could never figure out the reason, except maybe that everybody in law school was certifiably crazy and didn't want to get better. Type A that I am, though, I fell easily into the stream. The first year, I did what it took to get all A's.

With such good grades, there was only one path for me to take after law school: to wear a little grey suit and a little white blouse (but no bow tie, thank you). I was an attractive woman with an M.B.A. who could speak well, and I had good people skills. The firms fell all over me, and I chose to see my overwhelmingly warm reception as a sign that practicing law must be my life mission.

The first two weeks, I had insomnia, a bad cold and a rash. I walked around the office joking that I must be suffering from "I-don't-want-to-work-itis," but gave assurances that I just needed time to acclimate. Inside, though, I knew it was a mistake to be working there from the moment I walked in the door.

I was always stressed out. Ten percent of every day I spent bitching about my job or about someone else's. On top of it, everyone else was complaining about their work, too. The law firm system didn't make any sense. The partners continued to raise the salaries of associates while treating them badly. Associates got lots of financial perks but when it came to nurturing job satisfaction, the partners had no interest. The whole atmosphere wore me down.

One day, the woman in the next office who had been practicing with the firm for five years, confided that she wanted to make a change. When I confided the same thing, the two of us decided to stop complaining and start doing something constructive about our dissatisfaction.

I lasted two years. When I finally announced my resignation, there was a parade of associates streaming into my office to congratulate me and to admit that it was the money that stopped them from following in my footsteps. They were single, in their late 20's, and truly believed they couldn't survive on less than $50,000 a year. Even a firm partner, who I'd thought loved his work, told me that he wished he could do the same thing, but that with a wife and three kids he couldn't give up the money. I'm so glad I didn't share those values.

THE TIES THAT BIND

Danny Hoffman, a Stanford Law School graduate, has identified three progressive stages of dissatisfaction among young lawyers. He bases them on his own experience practicing law in Dallas, and conversations with others in his current avocation as a legal headhunter. Hoffman calls the first stage the "Houston Syndrome." It starts when second-year law students get wined and dined by out-of-town firms in order to induce them to accept a summer clerkship. The courtship continues all summer to persuade them to accept an associate position upon graduation. Once they agree, the wining and dining cease, and suddenly the new residents realize what an awful city they've chosen. Says Hoffman, "Houston is a hotbed for legal headhunters — Oklahoma too — because everyone wants to leave as soon as they get there."

In the second stage, Hoffman says the firm itself is the defined problem. Whether the result of a personality conflict with a partner or disgust with a department of glum workaholics — large firm or small — the unhappy associate begins looking for a more congenial environment. Job-hopping to resolve what seems like a problem of either geography or personality, the young lawyer soon concludes, as one disillusioned associate put it, that "I've had the same terrible job in two different buildings."[11] At that point, the third stage is reached: a dislike of law practice itself.

At the beginning of their careers, most lawyers are willing to endure almost any discomfort by anticipating the Big Pay-Off. Once they're established and financially secure, they begin to wonder what else they could do for a living. But, they get trapped by "golden handcuffs." San Francisco lawyer-novelist Walter Walker, working on his fourth book while again practicing law full time, admits, "If someone said I could make as much money writing as practicing law, I would quit law in a minute. But I make four times as much money lawyering as writing and I have a wife and two kids to consider."

For those who entered the profession to contribute to society, took low-paid public service positions, and are now earning salaries comparable to those paid to experienced legal secretaries, the thought of leaving generates tremendous guilt. Socially-conscious attorneys wonder who will be left to carry on the tradition of service if they, and others like them, leave the profession to those who see the work only as a way to earn money and prestige. Similarly, attorneys who want to minimize the strain of the legal system on their clients' lives, and thereby keep costs down, worry about abandoning their clients to less empathetic practitioners.

Guilt ties many women to the profession as well. Considering the barriers to success they must overcome, one would think women would find it easy to act upon their dissatisfaction by leaving the law. On the contrary, they must overcome even greater self-doubt than men before leaving the profession. Not only do they feel pressure to be role models and mentors for other women, but they sincerely believe that a feminine influence might somehow humanize the legal system. They trap themselves by anticipating (and oftentimes actually being the brunt of) criticisms: "You took the place of a man, or of another woman, in law school. How can you waste your education and training?" or "Women need other women to promote their interests in a male-dominated society."

Overall, the pull of the profession seems to go to the very center of the self-image of the men and women in it. Perhaps motivated to enter law school because of some belittlement in their earlier life — whether from parents, lovers or teachers — becoming a lawyer supplied just the right boost to their egos. Discarding their identity as a lawyer threatens to strip them of their self-esteem.

Aggravating the situation further, most veteran lawyers so identify with the profession that they seem unable to translate what expertise they have developed into talents which are transferable to another industry. For example, many trial lawyers are unable to redefine their experience in court, and facility in writing briefs, into such marketable skills as persuasive speaking and writing, research, organization and analysis.

Worse yet, lawyers must confront the realities of the marketplace. First of all, they are perceived in the corporate world as being argumentative, unimaginative and narrow-minded; personality characteristics likely to destroy the corporation's team-building and deal-making efforts. Some lawyers can prove that they are, indeed, team players by emphasizing their negotiation and case management skills. Then, they offer the rest of their legal experience as evidence of their intelligence, dedication, attention to detail and ability to perform well under pressure. But they still must contend with the prejudices of hiring personnel who refuse to believe that anything but failure would motivate a licensed attorney to apply for a job as a non-professional. A reporter from a major San Francisco newspaper, himself a licensed attorney who never practiced law, best represents this attitude. According to Hindi Greenberg, he inquired about her Lawyers in Transition organization by asking, "What kind of people are in this group? Are they all losers?"

Too often, family and friends reinforce this shortsighted perception, trying to convince unhappy lawyers that they are either crazy or foolish to give up the money, respect, prestige and years of investment in the profession. In this dilemma, practitioners are caught by a rigorous and limiting standard, something like being born into royalty; that, by assuming the privileges and responsibilities of the profession, they have also agreed to a lifetime tenure. "When you go into law, it doesn't occur to you that one day you're going to feel trapped," acknowledged a former practitioner at two prestigious law firms. "As committed as I was to leave, I had no way of knowing that I would hear my own inner voice tell me, 'You're a grown-up now. What do you mean you're going to leave the law?'"

Most lawyers also make the mistake of hiding their dissatisfaction from co-workers and colleagues. In fact, they are advised by their peers to do so. For example, the *ABA Journal* published an article entitled, "Things They Didn't Teach in Law School," which admonished young lawyers to be discreet about voicing their "dreams and dissatisfactions." Even though "it's normal to experience spells of doubt about your career choice, do not confuse friendliness with friendship and be especially careful about revealing anything personal to a partner."[12]

This advice is well taken. In recent years, the war mentality of the adversarial system, which defines as an "enemy" anyone who disagrees, has controlled law firm organizations. When an associate is unhappy, or makes suggestions for improvement to the system, that person takes the risk of being treated as a scapegoat. Or, they might face the response that Hindi Greenberg received when she requested an accommodation from the large San Francisco law firm for which she worked. "After handling piecemeal assignments for an oil antitrust case for six months, I was immediately assigned as the junior lawyer to six others on a case involving 117 other law firms. After a while, I went to the managing partner and asked to be moved into something that would give me better experience. He replied — without an opportunity for discussion — that the needs of the firm were that I continue to work on that case. So I quit."

In this closed environment, a disgruntled associate will seldom confide in those with the power to provide meaningful help. Attitudes of "if-you're-not-for-us-you're-against-us" or "we're-sorry-we-can't-do-anything-about-it-that's-just-the-way-things-are-here" encourage those who disagree with employee policies to plot their escapes in secrecy. In seeking to protect themselves from criticism, however, lawyers miss out on what would probably be a lot of grateful support from others who are equally afraid of confessing how unhappy they are. "When I announced that I was leaving a 225-person law firm in Chicago," says one former practitioner, now specializing in public relations for law firms, "other associates trooped into my office to tell me their life stories. They'd come in and shut the door and literally start crying. So many wanted to leave, too, but felt they couldn't."[13]

Instead, they keep quiet while their dissatisfaction festers. Some of them end up working in the profession for a lifetime while savoring only fantasies of a more fulfilling life. Without the courage, persistence and faith to plunge forward, the barriers to change loom even higher.

George earns a six-figure income after a dozen years of practice in matrimonial law. He says he wants to stop practicing law, but so far hasn't figured out how without turning his life upside down. What appeals to him is a career in psychological counseling. The trouble is, he insists on maintaining his income level, he's unwilling to return to school, and he hasn't committed himself to an all-out search for a more fulfilling career. Altogether, these choices keep *George* grinding away in the law.

◆

George's Profile

B.A., Cornell University, 1970
C.P.A., 1972
J.D., Boston College of Law, 1975
Currently, matrimonial law practitioner

George's Statement: I know lawyers in their 50's and 60's who admit they've suffered for the last 25 years, but not one of them has left. Most people around my age certainly question why they continue to practice. But, as much as they complain, they don't do anything, nor do they seriously consider changing.

I wasn't sure that I enjoyed law right from the start. But, I questioned whether my desire to leave was tied to doubts I had about being able to cut it. Ten years later, I feel I have represented people very well and have a good handle on how to do what I do. Nothing really throws me anymore. All in all, I feel a lot more confident. But, I still don't like it, and at age 39, I'm only now recognizing that there are other things I want to be involved with again. For example, my family. Or just taking the time to read a book once in a while.

What keeps me here is the pull of my practice. During the summer, I spent quite a few sessions with my career counselor, and was really making progress toward making the change. All of a sudden, three of my cases broke open. To prepare one case alone, I had to work 200 hours in only a few weeks. I couldn't devote time to looking for something else to do.

This happens periodically. A law practice is not the kind of work where I can say, "It will take me three weeks to finish this job, and then I can stop for three weeks and have time to look." The cases are going all of the time. Emergencies arise every day. This week, I finally could look forward to a couple of slow weeks . . . and then my secretary breaks her arm! Getting out of law is so hard. There's always something demanding my time.

Taking a sabbatical is too ambitious for me to even think about. It costs me well over $100,000 to run the office each year. If the money isn't coming in, there's still $10,000 per month going out. That kind of drain doesn't take very long to be a problem.

To me, money is important only to the extent that I can support a modest lifestyle. I don't feel that I need to make four times what I make, but I do need to make what I make now just to get by. It's a very high cost of living here. You can't touch a house that's decent for less than $400,000, and taxes are very high. When I talk about even a modest living, paying the mortgage, buying food, I have to make $80,000 to $100,000 a year.

As a young lawyer, I was working toward something. I wasn't sure what it was, but I was wetting my feet and that made practicing law more exciting. Now that the challenge is gone, my work bothers me more and more. But it's hard to get unused to things. Lifestyle is a big barrier to change.

GOLDEN HANDCUFFS

Even those who do divorce themselves from the profession continue to struggle with the money issue. The reason is simple. There's little else an experienced practitioner can do that matches law's potential for earning a respectable income so quickly and easily. As a result, no matter how many years have elapsed since their exodus from law, nearly all former practicing attorneys continue to maintain their licenses. In fact, inactive status bar association enrollment has increased dramatically across the country.[14]

Janna, like many other dropped-out lawyers, takes comfort in the knowledge that she can always practice law again if she should ever face monetary difficulties. In fact, she entered law school for just that guarantee: to obtain an education that would get her a job. After two attempts at big-firm practice, and one aborted escape from law, she finally extricated herself. But still, she is keeping her legal credentials safely up-to-date, to be drawn upon if she's hit by a financial emergency.

◆

Janna's Profile

B.A., Brown University, 1975
J.D., Boalt Hall, University of California, 1978
Associate, two corporate megafirms, 1978-85
Currently, fiction writer

Janna's Statement: I've always found myself pulled between doing what I want — with no concern about supporting myself — and being in financial control of my life. That's why I went to law school — to get a professional degree that I could use to earn a living. I figured law school would suit me better than other graduate programs because I presumed that it was geared to the generalist. But, I wasn't certain I would practice law when I applied. I just looked forward to the challenge, and I thought I would benefit from the training.

The whole law school experience, though, made it very hard to hold onto that vision. Once I got caught up in the competition and started winning, it was difficult to turn down the lucrative job offers, especially because all my friends were doing it. I got trapped by the status; something like wanting to get an invitation to a certain party whether or not you really want to attend.

I accepted a job at one big-name New York firm, telling myself that it would be a one-year stint. I was curious about the experience and also wanted to put a stamp on my degree before I did something else. But after a year, I was asked to go to the firm's Paris office — a plum appointment — and, as things turned out, it was the best thing that happened in my legal career.

After two years there, the firm insisted that I return to the New York office. Although I had developed a lot of confidence abroad, and some valuable skills, the work had already become meaningless and the hours were grueling, leaving little time for life outside the office. If my only goal had been to make a good, safe living, I'd have been able to put up with it. But I was miserable and I resigned. I told the firm that I had no other job lined up; I just didn't want to practice law anymore. The other associates thought I was nuts; not just for leaving, but for not playing my cards into an even more lucrative position in the business world. It was very hard for them to understand how I could give it all up.

I moved to Los Angeles for a job in the entertainment industry. Soon after that, I married, and moved to the San Francisco area where my husband had started a company. I joined a large San Francisco firm to support us while he got his business off the ground. I knew that the experience I'd gain, dealing with high technology start-up companies, would be helpful to my husband who was starting that type of business himself, and it certainly has been. But, the bottom line was, I took that job for the money.

Once my husband's business got going, and I inherited a bit of money, I was under less pressure financially. At that point, it seemed that I had no reason to keep practicing law. I wanted to spend more time writing, and I worried that if I stayed in law any longer, I would never get out. That's when I quit.

73

Even now, I feel confident that I could always go back to law in some capacity. But it's only if we needed the income, and I couldn't find anything more satisfying, that I'd consider it.

Making the Break

The best way out is always through.

◆

ROBERT FROST

P ractitioners can list all sorts of reasons to remain in the profession — intellectual challenge, money, respect, prestige, security. But for those no longer willing to pay the price for something they've grown to dislike, the process of disengagement is pretty straightforward.

First, unhappy lawyers must start to listen to their inner voice. For example, while preparing for a trial after 13 years of practice, *Barbara* heard that tiny voice inquire, "How many times do you have to go through this until you learn that you don't want to do it anymore?" In the case of *Mike*, who was 10 years into a thriving criminal defense practice in Oregon, he stopped one day to ask himself if he was enjoying his life and got back a resounding "Hell, no!"[1]

By studying lawyers around them, the unhappy lawyer may then develop the resolve needed to take action. "Some of my acquaintances — mostly trial lawyers from age 35 to 44 — could not understand my desire to stop," said one eight-year veteran from Portland, Oregon. "I couldn't explain it to them either. How did I say to a certain guy, 'You're on your third marriage. I don't want to be on my third marriage.' Or, to another, 'You're 37 and have a bleeding ulcer. I don't want to have an ulcer.' Or, 'You're 42 and you keeled over from a heart attack while running last Sunday. I don't want to do that.' But I knew I was not going to be the exception."

The pivotal point occurs when unhappy lawyers can clearly visualize a future away from law. Then, and only then, are they able to unlock their "golden handcuffs"... and create ways to survive, even thrive, on a temporarily suspended or reduced income. Some stash money away, or accrue enough equity in their law partnerships, to cover for a few years their living expenses. Others leave the profession as soon as they have secured alternate employment, either a full-time position in a new field or working part-time as a contract lawyer. A few rely upon the income of a working spouse. But no matter how they handle the financial arrangements, it is their vision of a more satisfying life after lawyering that keeps them motivated.

SEEING THE LIGHT

Barry held an enviable position as a senior partner of a prestigious New York law firm. After many years of working almost around-the-clock, his life had eased into a pleasant routine of practicing law by day and, in the evenings, painting and sculpting. But when a voice inside him announced the time to follow his passion in art, *Barry* was attentive enough to finally leave the law.

◆

Barry's Profile

B.A., New York University, 1958
J.D., New York University, 1961
Assistant U.S. attorney, 1961-64
Partner, commercial law firm, 1964-82
Currently, professional sculptor and painter

Barry's Statement: I wish I'd left law sooner. But like everything else, it happened at one of those times when I least expected it.

I was actually happier practicing law than I had been in years. My work load was much easier because I had more help. I was doing much more supervisory work rather than all the detailed stuff that used to consume me. Life was a lot better than it had been, but by then I had already crossed over the line.

I was on my way home from Norway, where I had obtained lengthy affidavits for an international bankruptcy matter. It had been a wonderful week, full of intellectual stimulation. But, when I was on the plane home, all of a sudden, I had this overwhelming feeling that I had to stop practicing law. Before that moment, one of my biggest barriers to leaving was that I could not walk away from my partners; that I owed it to everybody to stay put for the rest of my life. At that moment, though, it all became crystal clear; I knew exactly what I had to do, and how I would tell them. The relief was so great that I started to cry. That clinched it. There was no turning back.

When I practiced commercial law, I never had the sense I was doing anything of great social value. It was more a matter of getting satisfaction out of presenting the best legal case I could with the facts and legal precedent I had. Although the work was very challenging, it was also totally consuming. At first, we were a very small firm, and we worked harder than everybody else because we had to make up for the lack of numbers. The work load was incredible: seven days and seven nights at the beginning. It was a grind.

After the first seven years, I started to question what I was doing. So, as a way of expanding my life, I invested in an art gallery with three others. I participated in the planning, visited artists' studios and helped to select artists to represent. On weekends, I would go down to see what was going on. Before long, I began to read and study obsessively about art.

About a year after we opened the gallery, I started drawing after I came home from work, sometimes feeling so driven that I was at it until almost dawn. A few hours later, I'd go back to the office. The more I indulged my interest in art, though, the more frustrated I got with the life I was leading as a successful commercial lawyer. Other lawyers in the firm seemed totally obsessed with practicing law, that being the major impulse in their lives. And, with only a few exceptions, it seemed they didn't resent the demands because they weren't actively involved in anything else. On the other hand, my life was becoming schizophrenic. I tried to put my energies into the law as fully as I could, but art engaged me more and more.

Initially, I was just discontent. Then I started to realize how I was not living the kind of life that I really wanted to live.

Deciding whether or not to leave presented a multi-faceted conflict. On the one hand, there were the non-material rewards —

the excitement of cases; the intellectual challenge; the prestige of being with a successful firm; the good feeling of being accepted as a successful lawyer. There were also the material rewards. As unhappy as I was, those things were hard to give up.

On the other hand, I was really in love with, and excited by, painting and art, and I hadn't felt that way about law for a long time. I had this feeling that I could do something significant with my life by devoting myself to art. Sure, I had doubts about starting a new career. Was I fooling myself? Did I only want to escape from law, or did I truly believe that I could do something meaningful? Did I have enough money to make the change and still maintain a reasonable lifestyle until I established myself again? What would it mean to my family?

Most lawyers I know are extremely interested in hearing about others who have left the law because 95 percent of them have secret yearnings to leave themselves. The only advice I can give is that when you begin to be unhappy with what you are doing, take the time to isolate the reasons why. If you find that you can't change them, then leave.

People say I was courageous to do what I did. But leaving law was a necessity for me. It was like having an illness. The way I see it, I either had to cure myself, or watch a big part of me die.

COMMUTING A LIFE SENTENCE

Not all attorneys who leave the profession respond as quickly as *Barry* to urgings of their inner voice. Some don't take action until they've thoroughly worn themselves down. Career counselors and psychologists would probably label these attorneys victims of burnout — the exhaustion that comes from unrelieved stress. But those who have experienced it see it as something even more debilitating: battle fatigue. It's the despair that comes from generating piles of meaningless paperwork; the relentless obligations to clients and the courts; the long hours, the constant deadlines, the tremendous pressures, and the lack of positive feedback.

Some discontent manifests itself in the form of a chronic physical ailment, similar to that suffered by Arnold Patent, or a serious illness like

Sharon experienced in Chapter 3. In still other cases, lawyers risk a kind of emotional death evidenced by depression, alcoholism, or other substance abuse.

The moment of truth usually occurs when attorneys realize that they do not want to end up like so many of their peers: cynical, ulcer-ridden, depressed, divorce-prone, or worse — an obituary before their time. For example, *Kathleen*'s pivotal moment occurred while observing one of her superiors at an office party. "He was 50, but I noticed how he looked 20 years older than his age," *Kathleen* remembers. "And I thought to myself, 'I don't want to end up like John.'" Soon after, she dropped her position as a deputy district attorney to work toward something she always wanted to do — become a commercial airline pilot.

Although *Bolling* entered the legal profession with a crusading spirit, he was worn down by simple economic reality. Money came from handling cases and clients that would pay, not from trying to prove a point or representing the underdog. With the decline in civility among lawyers further dragging down his spirits, *Bo* decided to escape to the world of international commerce, and the promise of greater financial and psychic returns.

◆

Bolling's Profile

B.A., University of Virginia, 1968
Rhodes Scholar, Oxford University, 1971
J.D., Harvard Law School, 1974
Partner, midsize civil litigation firm, 1975-88
Currently, managing director of an international manufacturing
*   concern*

Bolling's Statement: When I chose law school, I was expecting a lifetime of romance, excitement, and heroic deeds. Really! It was so discouraging to find out how much of a grind it is; how hard you have to work even to become minimally proficient.

Law appealed to me originally as an "impact profession." I expected to use my law degree to integrate the schools, win civil rights suits and make the country safe for the Equal Protection Clause. I would be rabble-rousing with clients and civil rights

79

activists, going into court to win lawsuits which desegregated the state. I'd have my picture taken as I stood on the steps of the courthouse, making a big contribution while living a life of excitement. I expected law to be completely fulfilling.

Once I got into law school, nothing changed my perception that you could use the law to get things done on behalf of society. In fact, every year something happened that only confirmed my view that I was heading in the right direction. I worked for Ralph Nader. I clerked for a distinguished civil rights jurist. Our cases were on the cutting edge of law. I thought to myself, "How could anybody have picked a better profession than I did?" That's what I thought in 1974 and 1975. Nixon had just left office. The Democrats had won control of Congress in a big, big way. The Vietnam War was winding down. Saigon would fall in 1975. Not only had the legal process been instrumental in making those changes, it had been critical. I didn't see any reason why our society wouldn't continue to be driven by the same forces.

By the time I started practicing, though, the Movement was waning. The Civil Rights struggles were over; the draft had ended, and the war was winding down. I joined a firm which handled some environmental and civil rights work, but I discovered that what any firm has to do to survive is to process a lot of bread-and-butter cases — real first-year law school stuff — that are not as stimulating or fulfilling as I had naively anticipated.

I quickly figured out the business aspects of the law, maximizing the value of each case by minimizing the time I spent working on it. But still, I had to work horrendous hours to pay the rent. And look at the work! It's pushing paper. It's deadly dull. It's dehumanizing. It's dispiriting. It's so devoid of, and removed from, real human contact.

What makes it even more trying is the lack of courtesy and civility in the profession. Take depositions for example. Do you realize that lawyers spend a large part of life, from sun-up till sundown, trapped in rooms with people they don't like? Facing opposing counsel who are downright nasty, adversarial, rude, and obstreperous; witnesses who are either evasive or, worse, outright liars.

Then, these same attorneys head over to the courthouse and see people who are hostile, aggressive and uncivil; who act in a way they would never act anywhere else. And it's gotten worse. The way lawyers behave is as much a part of practicing law now as the issues being pursued. It takes a tremendous psychological toll to be involved in a business where there is so much unnecessary stress engendered by hostile interpersonal interactions and relationships.

And then there's the system itself. Eisenhower was a great general but he was not a great military strategist. What he did well was take people, tanks and planes and move them from point A to point B before the other side got there. He managed a war of attrition.

Litigation, too, is a war of attrition. Cases are handled like World War II, organizing the paralegals, associates, interrogatories and depositions, briefs and pleadings, and marching them off to the courthouse steps. These armies assemble at the courthouse door and then everybody realizes the system won't accommodate them. So the lawyers and judges enter into a conspiracy to settle the case before trial. The defense attorneys get their hours to bill. The attorneys for the plaintiff get their share of the client's settlement. The judges get some relief from court congestion. And the clients get relief from the ruinous expense and emotional wear-and-tear they can't bear any longer.

There's a con game going on. In essence, we don't have an adversarial system anymore because there's no location in which to have a true contest. But the lawyers carry on as if it is an adversarial system anyway, and, in that way, everybody gets compensated.

The legal profession deifies precedent, and procedure, and routine, and the whole traditional way of doing things. Change interjects too much anxiety into the system. As a result, lawyers are very conservative people. That's the whole psychology of the profession.

I never wanted to be a servant of corporate America, but law is a business and I am basically a business person who has developed some valuable entrepreneurial and managerial skills. If I'm not happy in law, I have to ask myself why I'm doing something so labor intensive with so little return per hour. Life is too short.

If the legal system could be rehabilitated over the next 10 or 15 years, that would be a challenge worth accepting. But I don't think the practice of law is going to change. And, if it can't be rehabilitated, I'm not going to stick around and get battered trying to fix it.

PLOTTING AN ESCAPE

Some attorneys respond to their inner signals with the same conscientiousness and attention to detail they applied to their lawyering. They carefully investigate other career possibilities, sometimes on their own but more often with the assistance of a professional career counselor. They might also consider consulting with a psychotherapist to be certain that their dissatisfaction has its roots in their environment and not in some deeper inner conflict.

Other practitioners work together to plot a reasoned path out of the profession. As an example, two San Francisco lawyers noticed how much time they spent grousing with co-workers about their work. Once they realized that their negative attitude was not going to create a better work environment, they made a pact with each other to take a moment each day to write down on their desk calendar the one thing they most enjoyed doing. Even this short mental break helped each of them to focus on what elements in a job would be more satisfying. Within a year, both of them had moved into equally respectable non-legal positions.

Those who are methodical about their leave-taking are in the minority. Still, their numbers are growing and, to help them, there are an increasing number of career counselors specializing in the law. Two career planning books designed especially for lawyers were published within the last year. And seminars about how lawyers can make the best use of their degrees and backgrounds are attracting lawyers in every major city.

For *Robert*, law school represented a continuance of his long-time drive toward achievement. After only a few years in the profession, however, and on a day he will long remember, *Robert* realized that while what he'd attained impressed others, it would never be personally satisfying. Once he was able to acknowledge that, he turned to a career counselor. With guidance and encouragement, *Robert* carefully plotted his departure from law.

Robert's Profile

B.A., Princeton University, 1979
J.D., Fordham Law School, 1982
Associate, large law firm, 1982-88
Currently, freelance development officer for performing arts
organizations

Robert's Statement: In 1987, I was working on a month-long project in Washington, D.C., when the associate review committee called me from New York to give me my annual critique. They said, "You're doing fine, blah, blah, blah, but you don't have enough initiative."

"There's a good reason for that," I wanted to say, "I hate doing this."

I realized then that I could only continue pretending for so long. I didn't like what I was doing, and it was bound to show one way or another. When I realized that, I began asking myself why a perfectly competent person like me was subjecting myself to criticism.

That very same day, I saw a copy of the *National Law Journal* with a front page article about lawyer dissatisfaction. It was a moment I'll always remember; an epiphany. The article appeared at the right time with the message I needed to hear: that I wasn't unusual, or alone, feeling as I did. That what I was feeling wasn't a flaw in my character. That the law is right for some people and not right for others. And that there were people I could look to for help.

Right then, I decided I was going to get out of law. I circled in red the names of the two career counselors mentioned in the article and investigated them the minute I returned to New York. My counseling sessions started in April, 1987.

We started out by talking about what I would do if I could do anything I wanted. Although I was suspicious at first, that exercise helped me understand that I like to solve problems, to nurture things and make them bloom into something. I don't like to fight, nor do I share those values held in high esteem by most lawyers — competition, aggressiveness, a fast pace, being considered an expert, or getting a case exactly right down to the last detail. I also came to realize that my creativity is severely restricted in law. My writing style is restricted by its conventions, and I can't be as emotional as I would like.

I enjoy writing, researching, and advising — things I do in law — but charging a lot of money to shift dollars around from one person to the next isn't enough to sustain me. What I need to do is work toward a purpose which transcends a corporation's goal of making money. From all that analysis, I've concluded that I want to work for a nonprofit organization, doing what I'm doing now, but without the fighting.

With my counselor's help, I've picked out a career that is more in tune with my interests, and personality, and overall values. And I've decided to quit my law job to look for other work. I've never taken a risk like that before. Now that I think about it, going to law school was a choice I made to avoid risk. By applying, I didn't have to think about finding a job, didn't have to worry about my student loan payments starting. I pushed off thinking about my life, my future and my interests.

I feel proud of myself because, at last, I've taken the time to figure out what I want to do with my life. I no longer want to be a lawyer by default. I'm prepared for the downsides, especially the financial loss. I make $75,000 a year now, but I'm willing to drop to $35,000.

I can't help but think about something my mother told me when I was in law school. I had said something like "I can't wait until the semester is over," and she asked me, "What are you going to do, wish your life away?" That's exactly what I've been doing here. I can't wait until this brief is done; can't wait until this case settles, or until this trial is over. I'm done wishing my life away.

SHOCK THERAPY

Some unhappy practitioners take all the right steps to find an alternative position: they consult with a career counselor, take vocational guidance tests, see a therapist. They analyze what they like and don't like about their work. They thoroughly explore other options within the law, and then finally decide to apply all their time and energy to a search for something more tailored to their personalities and needs. But they're thrown by what happens next.

The moment they give notice, they become professional pariahs. Their declaration of independence is often twisted into what their employers construe as an unforgivable affront to the firm. Shunned by their employers and perhaps even their peers, they're treated as if they had been fired. And sometimes, especially when they haven't decided what direction they want to move, they come to believe it themselves.

From the time *Valerie* was in grade school in the rural Midwest, her teachers encouraged her to pursue a college education. She heeded their advice, and followed the path recommended for honors liberal arts graduates — law school. Next, she listened to conventional law school wisdom that private law firm experience was the only way to become a skilled practitioner, and turned down more interesting offers to toil in the litigation department of a large corporate law firm. On the following pages, *Valerie* tells what happened when she finally confronted her mistake in following the advice of others.

◆

Valerie's Profile

B.A., Purdue University, 1976
J.D., Stanford Law School, 1979
Associate, corporate law firm, 1979-80
Currently, director of private family charitable foundation

Valerie's Statement: The two most thrilling days of my life were graduating from law school and being sworn into the bar. But when it came to actually practicing law, I was almost instantly miserable.

A friend of mine in whom I'd confided my dissatisfaction referred me to a job counselor. The first time I met with her, she said, "You are in the wrong place and need to be doing something different," and asked how soon I was going to leave. To tell you the truth, I don't remember whether she was suggesting that I leave law, or that particular firm, because to me it was one and the same.

My first reaction was to believe she was absolutely wrong. It was wrong to change jobs in less than two years. I needed stability. I needed the experience and income. But she countered with a long list of reasons why I shouldn't let that hold me back.

I was deeply confused by it all; embarrassed, too. And I was afraid to talk to anybody at the firm about it. Most of my friends from law school were living in other parts of the country, and my husband did not want to talk to me about it. He was jealous that I was a lawyer, and angry that I wasn't satisfied. I felt completely alone.

After visiting the therapist for a few months, I had a couple of pivotal experiences. One was spending a whole weekend trying to convince myself that I was doing interesting, important work; that a lot of people would really like to have my job. With that pep talk in my mind, I walked into the office Monday morning and ran into one of the other associates, who told me with great enthusiasm about a stock offering he was working on. I thought, "I've just spent 48 hours trying to fake what this guy genuinely feels."

A week or so later, I turned in something to a partner which was very badly done. He came in and bawled me out for it. After he left, I realized that I was (subconsciously) trying to get myself fired, and that it was a lot more honorable to quit. That insight came on a Thursday or Friday and I thought about it all during the weekend. On Sunday night, I wrote a letter giving two months' notice.

First thing the next morning, I handed it to one of the partners and he was livid. Even though I'd given two months' notice, he told me to be out of the office in two weeks. He also suggested that if there was anyone whose opinion I valued, I should talk to them soon because the rumors were going to start flying. For the next two weeks the guy tried to convince me that I had been fired. He told me my reputation was shot, and that no one would seriously look at me now. The only thing I could possibly do was go back to school and start over.

I believed him!

The first day or two after I was terminated, I found myself opening a beer before noon. I didn't know what else to do with myself. I couldn't go out of the house because people would see I wasn't in a suit. They'd know I was unemployed, and I couldn't bear that. I was so ashamed I even decided not to sit in the living room because it faced the sidewalk, and people would be able to see me sitting there. So, I sat in the back of the house.

After about a year of being severely depressed and mostly unemployed, I found an announcement at Stanford Law School for director of a new foundation in Palo Alto. The members of the board wanted a lawyer who could understand the regulations applying to non-profit corporations, yet someone new to the field who would help them shape their own agenda. It sounded like me. I applied, and got the job. I love it, and don't regret leaving law at all.

I guess the lesson you should take away from my story is: no matter how badly you handle a career change, you can get through it, and it can turn out very well in the end.

SCALING THE WALL

Hindi Greenberg, founder of San Francisco's Lawyers in Transition support group, has noticed a naïveté among many disgruntled attorneys. "A lot of people expect to hop from one job or career to another with a snap of the fingers. All of a sudden, a light bulb is supposed to turn on, their life path will be lit, and the perfect position will magically appear." But it doesn't work that way. Says Greenberg, "It is a long, arduous process." Traumatic as it may be, what many lawyers do not appreciate is how difficult the actual process of disengagement can be. The emotions connected with saying good-bye don't pass easily or quickly.

Drop-outs are usually struck by a wonderful sense of relief at first. An eight-year veteran described it this way: "I can't tell you how many times I woke up in the morning when I was practicing, and made a mental list of the things I dreaded that day, that week, that month; even three months down the road. It was a terrible way to start the day. The absence of that dread as a daily reality was the first thing I noticed."

Once this emotional high subsides, however, confusion often reigns. Larry Richard of *LAWGISTICS* attributes the problem to overidentification; that for some, law is not just a job, but an identity. "To be a lawyer, you go through a specialized process in three years of law school. You are taught how to think like lawyer. You endure a rigorous licensing process, work most of your waking hours on law, and then you're exposed to a population mainly of lawyers. It gets to a point where people ask who you are and you say, 'I'm a lawyer.' When you do decide to leave the profession, it's not like moving from IBM salesman to merchandiser of cable TV. It's a real loss of identity."

What follows for many is a crisis of confidence. Some attorneys experience the loss so profoundly that they plunge into a depression, lasting anywhere from several months to several years. "I didn't reckon on the confusion," one former high-powered corporate attorney conceded. "I thought I could make a transition much more easily. I was amazed at what quitting did to my self-esteem. I felt worthless."

If one believes that loss triggers depression, it is not surprising that many former practicing attorneys suffer. Leaving the profession activates a landslide of losses. Ex-practitioners sever longstanding relationships with partners and associates. Worse than that, their decision can alienate loved ones — spouses, children, parents, siblings — and perhaps even temporarily suspend their affection. Not infrequently, they lose the status and prestige associated with being a member of the legal profession. Equally sobering is the realization that, on its own, being a licensed attorney carries little weight in the job market. As one career counselor puts it, "Being a lawyer is a very specific box in society; easy to know and understand. Giving up that box is like losing your arm or your spouse."

Some ex-practitioners are totally bewildered by their doubt and confusion. "I felt completely committed to my decision," said one dropout from Los Angeles. "All the same, I felt I had let someone down. Should I have stayed in law instead of doing something I really wanted to do just so I could say I made partner? Would it look like I left because I wasn't sure I could cut it?"

Self-imposed isolation compounded his feelings of depression. "I did not talk about a lot of this stuff before I left. There was nobody in my life going through a similar process. Maybe that was one of the reasons it was so hard. I felt nobody understood. My family didn't understand. My wife didn't want me to cut off my options. I didn't know anybody who thought my quitting law was a decent idea. It seemed to me that I was totally out of step with the rest of the world."

Mary Kay was traumatized by resigning from her position as second-in-command of a major West Coast district attorney's office. But, like many other former practitioners, she softened the blow by taking what she considered an interim position as a clinical education instructor at a nearby law school. "Quitting the prosecutor's office was leaving law for me," she admits today. "Teaching was a way to earn an income while I figured what to do next." Three years later, *Mary Kay* finally mustered enough courage to abandon her carefully cultivated identity.

◆

Mary Kay's Profile

B.A., Gonzaga University, 1965
Schoolteacher, Brookline, Massachusetts, 1966-68
J.D., University of Washington School of Law, 1975
Deputy prosecuting attorney and chief criminal deputy, 1975-83
Clinical law instructor, 1983-86
Currently, full-time graduate student in clinical psychology and
*   operator of North Cascades Llama Company*

Mary Kay's Statement: Like most of us who ended up being lawyers, I performed well my whole life. I was usually class president or a cheerleader — an "all American girl" in a sweet little Catholic setting. There is no doubt in my mind that's why it ended up being so hard to give up law. It was awfully hard to get off that track.

When I was appointed Chief Criminal Prosecutor, I was quite young; not in age as much as in experience. That made the promotion very heady stuff. I thought it would be a satisfying change. But from the moment I took the job I hated going to work in the morning.

For the first six months I told myself, "Look, it's a new job. Maybe you're just feeling stressed by the change." But it became increasingly clear that I didn't like being an administrator at all. I missed the day-in, day-out contact with the women and children who were crime victims, and with the deputy prosecutors when we

89

tried to figure out evidentiary problems on cases. I missed the excitement of the unusual or very politically sensitive cases; the ones in the public eye.

I thought a lot about going back to being chief of the Sexual Assault Unit. But I had this idea that people shouldn't go backwards, and that maybe it wouldn't work out. I searched for people who had made a change such as the one I was contemplating — who had moved down the ladder of success, so to speak. I tried to find people from whom I could get reinforcement.

I took on enormous guilt for wanting to reject my promotion. I felt guilty that people who had been in the office longer than me had been passed over. I felt guilty because the people I confided in said things like, "You can't quit. It wouldn't be fair to your boss who stuck his neck out when he gave you the job," or "It's incredible that a woman is in this job. You have to stay there." I felt that I had to do it; but I couldn't. It was as if all the rulemakers in my life, the people who told me to succeed, were standing around me saying, "You're going to do *what?*"

I was getting no reinforcement from anybody. There was nobody else — except my therapist and a close friend or two — who told me it was okay to quit. I spent an extremely long time being depressed, fearful, overwhelmed and ashamed about wanting to get out of that appointment. Finally, I agreed to go into private practice with another attorney in the prosecutor's office, and then worked up the courage to resign. Right away, the press started sniffing around, wanting to know whether I'd been fired, and hoping to find a scandal.

Immediately after I quit, I spent a month in Washington State's North Cascade mountain range, thinking about my future. I spent a lot of time figuring out what I liked and didn't like, and might like in the future. What I liked was dealing with the victims and being in trial. What I didn't like was practicing law — negotiating with other attorneys, contending with the advocation of absurd positions designed only to waste time. I came back from my month off and, this time truly feeling like a flake, told the woman who was to become my law partner that I'd decided not to go into a partnership with her after all.

I don't know how to explain this, but I was so ashamed of quitting my job. Deep down inside, I believed that I had done something so wrong that, even now, I get choked up talking about it. I could hardly walk by the courthouse because I was afraid of running into judges on the street. I told my therapist, who had her office in that area, that I wanted to wear a cloak so I could sneak in. That's how awful I felt about it. I felt like it was, I don't know, like it was a sin to quit my job.

Then I got a pretty good offer for someone who didn't know what to do next. A colleague talked me into teaching at a local law school. Even there, though, I struggled internally. One morning, I was hosting a table of 10 or 12 at an alumni breakfast when the subject turned to how much we all hated the law. It absolutely boggled my mind. These lawyers were all in different areas of practice, out of law school for different numbers of years, and every single one admitted serious unhappiness with the profession.

I don't know very many lawyers who *are* happy. I think I know why. Law is an ungiving profession. It takes and takes and takes, and gives almost nothing in return. You get everybody else's problems heaped on you. You get enormous stress because every day you set out into an arena where somebody out there is trying to undo everything you are doing, or make you look like a fool. You are either going to be dealing with immediate difficulties or guarding against future ones, always with this idea that maybe you didn't quite do enough to avoid a future battle.

Law takes away a person's humanity. It starts with law school training where students are taught to advocate any position; to separate moral issues from legal issues. Your humanity and sense of right and wrong get whittled away. That's what I mean when I say the profession takes and takes. It takes away peace of mind.

I got interested in pack animals when I injured my back in a car accident the year before I stopped teaching. I couldn't carry a backpack anymore, so I started joking that the guy who hit me was going to have to buy me a llama. My back didn't heal and I missed being in the back country, so I started to research llamas and the market for their use. When I realized that there were a lot of other people out there like me — people who love to hike but can't carry

91

a pack — I convinced my best friend, another lawyer, to start a pack animal hiking service with me.

I feel like I had to be driven to get where I am today. Otherwise, I don't think I ever would have bought the idea of quitting law to move to the mountains. I'm glad I got here, but there's no question that I did it out of my own desperation.

Assuming a New Identity

He who gains a victory over other men is strong; but he who gains a victory over himself is all powerful.

◆

LAO-TSE

C elia Paul, who has been counseling attorneys for the last six years, believes that the education, training and wisdom that lawyers have at their disposal offer them an almost infinite number of employment opportunities. "There is almost no area some lawyer has not tried," says Paul. "Attorneys have developed successful businesses with no more background than just their ability to think on their feet, handle pressure, and set priorities."

For example, in 1988, Andrew Cuomo, son of New York Governor Mario Cuomo, quit his $225,000 per year law partnership to develop housing for the homeless at an annual salary of under $60,000. "I believe in my heart and soul," said Cuomo, "that this is the right thing for me to do."[1] And consider these other high-profile former practitioners:

- Ralph Nader, leader of a powerful national consumer watch-dog group.
- Richard Thalheimer, president of The Sharper Image retail chain.
- David Leiderman, owner of David's Cookies in Manhattan.
- Herbert D. Kelleher, founder, chairman, CEO and president of Southwest Airlines.
- Terry Louise Fisher, co-creator of NBC's "L.A. Law," the popularity of which some observers have given credit for an

astounding 18 percent increase in law school applications from 1987 to 1988.[2]

There are abundant examples of attorneys who have made successful transitions. On the pages that follow are some typical, and some of the more creative, paths taken by lawyers sincere about finding fulfillment in their work lives.

CORPORATE

Many lawyers decide to make use of the business and management skills they have developed. *Bolling*, featured in Chapter 5, accepted an offer to assume the managing directorship of an international manufacturing company after realizing that "law is a business, and I am basically a business person who has developed some valuable entrepreneurial and managerial skills."

Corporate Marketing. At first, *Cheryl*, a 1983 graduate of Northwestern University, loved her job as an associate in a large Chicago law firm. She worked directly for one partner and received a lot of hands-on experience with deals. Over time, however, she found herself more interested in the clients' businesses than in her own. "Law was only one part of the picture, and I wanted to be part of the big picture." After nearly three years practicing law, she took a job in marketing for Kraft, Inc., the food packaging giant. "When you work and socialize only with other lawyers, you lose sight of the fact that you're special in the job market," says *Cheryl*. "Employers look at you a little bit differently because you're a lawyer, and I think that enhances your ability to get hired. Legal training is a good springboard to do almost anything else you want to do.[3]

Entertainment Industry Executive. Peter became fascinated with the entertainment industry in the process of working on motion picture tax shelters. That fascination, combined with his role in setting up a public offering for the company which produced *Rambo*, resulted in an appointment as the firm's president and chief executive officer. "Practicing law prepared me in so many different ways for what I'm doing now," says *Peter*. "For example, when you work on a case, it's important not just to find the best solution to a problem, but to be able to evaluate risks and expectations, the same skills I use now."[4]

Headhunting. Lisa began her legal career in the high-pressure areas of oil and gas shelters and municipal representation. After only one year, she recognized that she would not be able to satisfy her commitments to the firm while also starting a family. Believing that a transfer into a corporate legal department would be more conducive to her family goals, *Lisa* visited Laura Colangelo, another former practitioner who runs a successful legal headhunting agency in New York City. Instead of finding *Lisa* another law job, though, Colangelo suggested that she join her headhunting firm. *Lisa* declined, but returned soon after the birth of her first child. Now, she acts as "handholder, psychologist, career counselor, matchmaker, and mother to attorneys, all rolled into one." Working only three days per week, she earns more than she would if she were practicing law part-time.

Manager of Human Resources. Sarah had spent five years doing employment litigation in a fairly large New York firm and was eager to leave. "All I knew was, I hated working at a law firm. I did not want to do it for another minute, never mind the rest of my life." Even after completing a career evaluation process, *Sarah* was still confused about her direction. Then, she noticed an ad in her alumni bulletin for a position as manager of employee relations at a national communications company. "When I was in private practice, I remember entering my office in the morning, looking at my watch, and thinking, 'Oh, my God, how am I going to get through the rest of today?' Now, from the minute I walk into my office in the morning until I leave at night, I don't think about anything but this business. The phone is constantly ringing, new issues constantly arise, and I love every minute of it. Time just flies."

Investment Banker. As an associate at Skadden, Arps, Slate, Meagher & Flom in New York City, *Donald* loved being a lawyer, but didn't like the day-to-day drafting of briefs and the supervision of paralegals. Three-and-a-half years later, he moved to Bear Stearns & Co., one of the nation's leading investment banks. "I wanted to get into the deal-making," says *Donald.* "But I wouldn't be completely honest if I said that the financial rewards weren't attractive too."[5]

Mergers and Acquisitions Specialist. In 1984, *George* left a high-pressure Manhattan law firm to join the First Boston Corporation as a specialist in mergers and acquisitions. His new six-figure salary was not the sole consideration for moving. It was the chance to do fascinating work. "Law practice has a few high spots," says *George*, "but it's primarily paperwork, research and exacting discipline to cover every base." As an investment banker, he adds, "I have more control over what I do, and the fast pace and turnover of deals is exciting."[6]

Planned Giving Manager. Mark spent six years working in a Manhattan insurance defense firm, and one year as corporation counsel for the City of New York, before responding to a classified advertisement in the *New York Law Journal.* The ad read, "University seeks attorneys. Estate, pension, trust experience preferred but not essential." At that point, *Mark* was "frenetic and frustrated" enough to consider anything outside of litigation. To his surprise, though, the job was not for an in-house counsel position but to work as a non-practitioner in the planned giving department of New York University. When he discovered that the job was totally outside law, he thought for an hour and then said to himself, "Sure. Why not?" Even without the preferred legal background, *Mark* impressed his future employers with his ability to learn what was needed. And, because of that same background, he was hired at nearly the same salary he earned in law. Now happily ensconced as manager of the department, *Mark* revels in an intellectually stimulating, but more relaxed environment. "Tonight is the first night in the six months of my son's life that I am not with him all evening. Enough said!"

Stationery Sales. With a family background steeped in law, *Debbie* had chosen law as her birthright and obligation. But *Debbie's* personality — outgoing, enthusiastic, with little interest in tedious details — makes her a natural born saleswoman. After a few years practicing alongside the most renown criminal defender in town, *Debbie* decided to apply her natural talents to the other side of the desk, selling office supplies to lawyers and other businesses. Says *Debbie*, "Rarely does a week go by that someone doesn't ask to pick my brain about leaving the law. Naturally, I'm happy to provide solutions and inspiration."

Stockbroker. David was a veteran Los Angeles lawyer who eventually became a stockbroker because the law "didn't leave a lot of room for creativity." Researching stock market trends, and managing his own portfolio, simply became more interesting and profitable than practicing law. Now, *David* manages client portfolios worth about $12 million. "This is a business in which my total compensation and wealth-building does not depend on my being in lockstep with a bunch of my peers," says *David*. "What I make depends on my output and what I contribute."[7]

Commercial Real Estate Sales. Near the end of his 10 years of practice in Maine, *John* successfully represented a client accused of murdering his wife. Disheartened by the jury's verdict ("It's hard to believe the act was not intentional, when you are staring at your victim's face and strangling her"), *John* left for an extended cross-country vacation. His reflections ultimately motivated him to leave the law, and head for the West Coast and a career in commercial real estate. "If I hadn't left law, I probably would have ended up in one of those fun one-car suicides," says *John*.

ENTREPRENEURIAL

Strict rules and procedures, and the avoidance of risk, make up much of the practice of law. But some practitioners crave excitement and speculation, and want to shape their own environments. From this group emerge the entrepreneurs. For example, a 1967 UCLA Law School graduate stopped practicing law in 1984 to become a successful theatrical producer. His latest production, *Romance/Romance*, received five Tony Award nominations. Another practitioner, this one from San Francisco, worked for about six years as an intellectual property specialist in a large law firm. Now, she designs on-site intellectual property protection systems for a variety of high-tech businesses in the San Francisco Bay Area. A member of yet another prestigious law firm made use of his legal background representing a nuclear energy company, and launched a monthly magazine that examines the effects of energy policies on consumers for an audience of utility and government decision-makers.

Still other practitioners parlay their knowledge of the legal system into jobs which serve lawyers. For example, one three-year veteran of a prestigious West Coast firm resigned along with three of his associates to start a small law practice. Once there, he became much more interested in computerized office management than in his caseload, and his interest in computer programming blossomed into the design of a software product and the formation of Terosoft Legal Software Company. Another associate in the same firm also bailed out of law. Her path included the purchase of a family construction business with her husband. Then, when the liability insurance crisis threatened to undermine the company's future, she founded a contract lawyer placement agency.

Jewelry Designer and Distributor. For almost 14 years, *Bill* held a variety of high-profile, law-related positions in Juneau, Alaska. As the legal profession became increasingly more complicated, however, *Bill* grew increasingly dissatisfied with his work. In 1981, he decided to sort things out by taking a sabbatical in Italy. There, it dawned on him that he could combine the knowledge he'd gained practicing law with the painting and drawing that he'd been doing his whole life. Now, he has his designs produced as decorative pins, and distributes them to museum shops and gift stores across the United States. *Bill* admits that his legal background frequently comes in handy in running this profitable business. But he's also quick to point out that being an entrepreneur is "miles more satisfying than sitting in an office strategizing about tax avoidance."

Computer Consulting and Training. *Carol* enjoyed her first two years of practice as a staff attorney with the National Organization for Women. When funds ran out for NOW's Legal Defense and Education program, *Carol's* position ended. Over the next few years, she became associated with a couple of small Manhattan law firms. In both offices, she was faced with "unrealistic expectations." As an associate, she was supposed to make life immediately easier for the partners, without any training and without being able to use their complicated computer systems. She was miserable, but out of her misery came a discovery: that automation — not hiring more and more associates — was the key to increased law office efficiency. Suddenly, she knew how she could find challenging work *and* be appreciated. *Carol* now acts as a self-employed consultant. She not only trains law firm clerical and professional staffs to make full use of the expensive computer systems they've acquired, but she also teaches computer vendors how to communicate effectively with lawyers.

Landscape Gardener. *Steve's* sense of social responsibility led him into law school, but his dream faded in the day-to-day realities of practicing law. "I spent my days writing letters, making calls and nagging," he says. When *Steve* announced his intention to become a landscape gardener, his family and friends wondered "whether there was some defect in my personality, or whether I didn't have the brains to make it as a lawyer." Now, *Steve* enjoys the creativity of designing environments on the steep slopes of Laguna Beach, California. What especially appeals to him is the ability to solve problems quickly. "It's not like lawsuits that can drag on for five years." Since winter business is slow and he earns upwards of $50,000 a year anyway, *Steve* spends the short days of the year reading and listening to music — hobbies he had little time for as a lawyer.[8]

Real Estate Developer. Tom spent six years working out deals between developers and neighborhood groups, but his law practice never interested him as much as the projects he was hired to protect. In 1981, *Tom* switched hats by joining his uncle in developing an office building. "A lawyer's job is to look at a project and see everything that can go wrong," says *Tom.* "A developer looks at a project and sees everything that can go right. I didn't want to be torn in two directions, so I dropped the lawyer part." In the last six years, *Tom* has acquired a portfolio of well over a million square feet of offices, hotels, warehouses and apartments with a market value of nearly $100 million.[9]

Maps to Movie Stars. To say that *Jack* took a cut in salary in giving up a 22-year corporate law practice would be, in his words, "a great understatement." But, as he neared age 50, *Jack* decided to "maximize my pleasure in life, not my net worth." That was five years ago. Today he owns and runs a small, bustling company that caters to Los Angeles tourists and film buffs. It's called Hollywood on Location, and he publishes a daily guide for finding and watching on-location movie productions. *Jack* enjoys his work, but says he's now even more prepared to "chuck it" again if something else catches his interest.[10]

Seminar Company Founder and President. Barbara, a 1974 gradu-ate of New York University Law School, spent five years litigating in a private law firm and the next four years as a staff attorney for the *New York Times,* "trying to figure out what I really wanted to do." While employed by the newspaper, *Barbara* realized how little practical information about libel and privacy laws was available to journalists. Fired by a need "to make a significant contribution, and to have some fun," she decided to package a series of seminars to news people, and designed them to make libel law both useful and interesting. In 1986, she also published *The Journalist's Handbook on Libel and Privacy*, and is now looking into extending her seminars into the area of avoiding medical malpractice claims.[11]

COMMUNICATIONS

Many lawyers transfer their writing, investigation, problem-solving and organizational skills into communications jobs, taking them into creative writing, reporting, public relations or publishing. In Washington State, three former practitioners now write for a popular regional newsmagazine, the *Seattle Weekly*. In California, Ralph Warner co-founded and oversees Berkeley's Nolo Press, America's first self-help legal publisher. And in New York, Kevin Ward was asked to join, and later direct, a corporate communications company in Manhattan after publishing *Not the Official Lawyer's Handbook*,[12] a satirical look at the legal profession.

Freelance Writer. As a litigator in Manhattan, *Gayle* regularly worked 12 to 14 hours per day as well as many weekends. After nine years with little free time, she traded a near six-figure salary and a secure practice for the uncertainty of a career as a freelance writer. "With my old schedule, things I was interested in fell to the wayside," said *Gayle*. "Now I play music, attend concerts, and I'm renovating my house. I'm more in control of my life."[13]

Humor columnist. As an associate with a Washington, D.C. communications law firm, *Rick* "was writing pretty much on the sideline." Then, for several years he acted as a legislative assistant, a position he got because he was "a lawyer who could write." After seven years, *Rick* abandoned the legal profession for something more fulfilling, and certainly funnier. He put down his briefcase to become a social and political satirist. His column now appears in over 30 newspapers around the country.[14]

Journalist. Joe quit his four-year corporate law position to do something he always wanted. He enrolled in Northwestern University's journalism program, and, after graduating, became a legal affairs reporter for the *Duluth News Tribune and Herald*. "I had secured a thoroughly safe financial setting but didn't really enjoy what I was doing," he explained. "I had to decide whether to put up with the unhappiness in exchange for the money, or get out."[15]

Newspaper Publisher. After 20 years of practice, *Arnold* found himself arriving later and later to work, and coming home earlier every day. In 1988, with no previous journalism experience, he gave up the status, prestige, and money of his law career to purchase and run the *Malibu Times*, a weekly community newspaper. What clinched his decision was meeting the man who had run it for 42 years. "He had good health and was happy!" *Arnold* told his legal colleagues he was buying a newspaper, and all they wanted to know was how he accomplished it, and how they might do it too. His only recommendation to them was that they accept the risk of change. "There's nothing worse," says *Arnold*, "than not wanting to get out of bed in the morning."[16]

Public Relations. Only a few months after graduating from the University of Michigan Law School, *Liza* began to have misgivings about practicing with one of Chicago's largest law firms. "I wasn't doing things I felt I was good at," she said. "I was in the library a lot, writing briefs, and had no sense of what was going on in the real world." She resigned from the firm without another job, and later found work as a law firm specialist with a national public relations firm. "The hours and the pressures are all less. Even the salary," says *Liza*. "But I have no regrets. At first, it tore me up to leave the profession, but I'm much happier now."[17]

Novelist. As a top entertainment lawyer in Los Angeles, *Ronald* had turned down a number of offers to be an executive in the film industry. Instead, he chose to write fiction in his spare time. Eventually, one of his spy novels was made into a movie. Still later, he wrote screenplays for such films as *Black Widow* and *Gardens of Stone*. Although his hobby became a thriving alternate career, *Ronald* postponed a full commitment to writing until his law partners assured him that they would welcome him back if he chose to return. "Writing freed me to use emotional parts of myself I had never tapped," admits *Ronald*. "It's like being a kid in a candy store. I'm actually getting paid for something I've always wanted to do."[18]

Movie and Television Scriptwriter. For the fun of it, *David* wrote the screenplay, *From the Hip*, while practicing as a litigation associate with a Boston firm. By coincidence, one of the firm's clients was a film production company, and before long, *David's* script was read and optioned. Even before the movie was made, though, *David* heard that producers of a new television series on lawyers were looking for writers. Because he found the mechanical and administrative functions of practicing law "unappetizing," it took *David* "only about a minute-and-a-half" to decide to take a leave of absence from his job to join the writing staff for NBC's "L.A. Law."[19]

Television Producer. Despite an abiding fascination with the law, *Harvey* realized after four years that, "practicing law just didn't turn me on." "I liked being in court," he says. "But since that's just a small part of what you do, I knew it would eventually become a problem." So *Harvey* combined his interest in law with another great passion — investigative journalism — to become a reporter on the criminal justice system for Los Angeles' KNBC-TV, and then, producer of "People's Court." "I use the law every single day of my life," says *Harvey.* "I make no apologies for wanting to entertain because, in every case, viewers walk away with some useful legal information."[20]

RE-EDUCATION

Most practitioners are loathe to endure any more schooling after completing their legal education and at least one bar examination. But those who do choose to explore teaching or psychological counseling as a next career often find further formal training to be essential. Stephen Feldman, a licensed psychologist featured in Chapter 2, funded his doctoral program at the University of Nebraska by teaching part-time at their law school. Another practitioner has reduced her law practice to four days per week to make time for a masters program in psychology.

Teaching via a Masters Degree. Ranald was earning a six-figure income as a tax lawyer in Anchorage, Alaska, but decided to enroll in Columbia University's Teachers College graduate program. A 42-year-old coal miner's son, *Ranald* knew he would take a substantial cut in pay as a teacher, but says he wearied of the 80-hour weeks and the cynical view of human nature that he felt was inherent in tax law. "I was not willing to spend another 25 years doing something a very immature person of 21 — me — had decided to do," says *Ranald.* "There's a limit to the satisfaction one can earn making a lot of money. I found the world could get along without one more good tax lawyer. But there are a lot of kids out there who might not do so well without a good teacher."[21]

Psychological Counseling via a Masters in Psychology. Garry practiced law for 20 years, working in a variety of environments — from the Legal Aid Society of Cleveland to the Pennsylvania Human Relations Commission; from the Equal Employment Opportunity Commission to private practice. In the aftermath of his sister's death in 1982, *Garry* began to struggle with the idea of getting out of law. One Sunday a few years later, he read a newspaper article about men changing careers in their 40's and decided that life was too short to spend it unhappily. The next day, he enrolled in a class on "Effective Therapeutic Communication" and, in time, earned a master's degree in psychology. He now is developing a one-on-one counseling practice. "When I first started in law school, I felt I could better the world as a lawyer," says *Garry*. "But lawyering is not about truth, justice and fairness. It's really about power and making money. I lost my idealism when I realized that law was not a panacea for all the problems of the world, and that I really wasn't making a contribution."

Psychological Counseling via a Ph.D. in Psychology. Tom was part of the wave of "crusaders" who entered law school in the 1960's. When he left, his grades earned him a coveted spot with the Federal Trade Commission. For three years, his work week consisted of reading a lot of magazines, and occasionally visiting a business to investigate charges of misrepresentation or fraud. When *Tom* finally tired of the lack of challenge, he moved to the Securities and Exchange Commission. It was even more boring, since he had no head for business. Out of the blue, he was offered a teaching position at a Midwest law school which gave him access to an alternative education program in the undergraduate school. Contact with that curriculum led him to an interest in studying human behavior. He then entered a Ph.D. program in psychology. Since 1980, *Tom* has focused his counseling practice on men struggling with relationships.

CAPITALIZING ON A HOBBY

The most satisfying farewell to the profession comes from those who capitalize on their hobbies to create non-traditional employment. *Mary Kay*, an avid backpacker featured in Chapter 5, permanently injured her back in an automobile accident. Unable to carry provisions for overnight hikes, she joked that the people responsible for the accident would have to buy her a South American llama to compensate her. And that's exactly what she did with the insurance settlement she received. Since then, her interest in llamas has led her to join forces with her co-worker, *Linda*, another high-country aficionado featured in Chapter 3, to found North Cascades Llama Company, a mountain guide service which totes gourmet meals and supplies for extended backpacking trips.

Transformational seminar designer and facilitator. Jerry, a 1966 graduate of Hastings Law School, admired his best friend's older brother because he went to Cornell, had an ROTC uniform in his closet, and wanted to be a lawyer. *Jerry* decided to follow in his footsteps, and never deviated. "I've always been a lawyer type," he says. "When I want something, I cross-examine like a guided-laser, heat-seeking missile, continuing until I get what I want . . . or piss the other person off." To *Jerry*, criminal defense work was a "fun game," until he realized that his job "was to make black look white." Before long, the fun had gone out of the game. "And then I began to resent it." His resentment motivated him to propose, and successfully present, a number of public interest programs ranging from a breakfast forum to a hand-holding for peace. In 1980, he created the Frog-Prince Conspiracy, a workshop designed to open the lines of communication between men and women. *Jerry* sums up the difference between practicing law and developing his workshops: "As a lawyer, I divided; now I join. As a lawyer, the game was always win/lose; now everything is win/win. As a lawyer, my relationships were all fleeting and superficial. Now they last."

Channeler. Kim devoted six years of her life to the defense of indigents. She believed then, as she does today, that the criminal justice system as it has developed in the United States is the only way to preserve the rights and freedoms of the accused in America. But working within that system drained her emotionally. Eventually, her body was attacked with daily headaches, tense, rock-like muscles and, despite a healthy diet, plenty of exercise and meditation, she was in a constant state of fatigue. In 1987, *Kim* resigned from her job to take a spiritual time-out. During that time, she recorded thoughts conveyed to her by her spirit "guide." Those writings are now a book, *Sojourns of the Soul: A Guide to Transformation.*[22]

Underwater Diver-Planner. Dace graduated from Harvard Law School in 1975 and went to work for the Los Angeles City Attorney. A few years later, she moved to Seattle, working for the city council as a specialist in land-use law. On a whim, she took a scuba class and traveled with some friends to dive the Great Barrier Reef in Australia. Before long, she became an avid scuba enthusiast. She kept diving, took an advanced course in marine law, studied marine biology and planned a trip to the Cayman Islands. There, she struck up a chance conversation with a local who told her the colonial government needed someone with a rather unusual set of credentials — a lawyer who was an experienced diver who could monitor and implement coastal land use controls in the Cayman Islands. Says *Dace*: "I know it sounds like an awful lot of lucky coincidences. But the difference is, I was looking."[23]

Commercial Airline Pilot. For six years, *Kathleen* spent her week days battling in court as one of the first female prosecutors in her county. Nights and weekends she devoted to piloting more and more sophisticated airplanes. When *Kathleen* took a good look at the mental and physical conditions of her superiors and realized how sorry they all looked, she grabbed a unique, but poorly paid, opportunity: combination in-house corporate counsel and corporate airplane pilot. That first pilot job led to another until she had accumulated enough commercial flight time to qualify as a flight engineer for United Airlines. There 10 years now, she has since earned a promotion to co-pilot. "I'm living everyone's dream," says *Kathleen*. "I'm doing the thing that I most enjoy doing and getting paid well for it too!"

No Remorse

There is no security on this earth; there is only opportunity.

♦

GENERAL DOUGLAS MACARTHUR

One question many lawyers put to ex-practitioners is whether they regret the choice they made to leave. Some want that last bit of encouragement before they, too, get out of the profession. But more often, the question is posed simply to confirm that maybe, just maybe, staying put makes sense. To hear Kevin Ward, though, lawyers contemplating leaving should get out while they can. On his worst days now, as head of a New York corporate communications company, Ward likes to remind himself that he could *still* be practicing law.

That's not to say that former practicing attorneys don't have some regrets about the way they left, or when. In hindsight, they might have accomplished their career change more efficiently, with less trauma, or with more support from others. Or, they might have left sooner, with more money or more direction, or with fewer conflicts. But, without exception, they all acknowledge that their decision to leave the law was among the best choices they have ever made.

Alan certainly expresses no remorse about leaving the profession. Involved in real estate development for over six years, *Alan* loves what he is doing; it is his passion. Not only does he have time to enjoy his young family, but he gets a kick out of the characters who inhabit the industry. Most rewarding to him, though, is the challenge that comes from investing his creativity, time and ingenuity where the potential for a large financial return is so great. His *only* regret is that he didn't get out of law sooner.

Alan's Profile

B.A., University of Virginia, 1967
J.D., University of Pennsylvania, 1970
Partner, securities law firm, 1970-82
Currently, real estate developer

Alan's Statement: It's been six years since I left. I can't get over how quickly the time has passed.

I don't regret having gone into the practice of law, or even having stayed long enough to get some sense of what it was about. And I have no regrets about leaving. None. Not for a minute.

What I do regret is having practiced for as long as I did. It irritates me that, in 10 or 11 years of practice, I probably put in four or five years too many. What tied me to the law for so long? My perception is that people either have stable relationships or they don't. I do. I've been married for almost 20 years. I worked with lawyers I liked. No one was driving me away from law. I was under no compulsion to get out of the practice. Unlike some of my friends, I was not unhappy. But I didn't feel great about practicing law. It wasn't fulfilling. And, it got boring.

Before I entered law school, I had no idea what lawyers did. I had no lawyer-mentors or other examples to follow. My mentor was my father. He was a good businessman in a small town sort of way; he ran a garage and fixed cars. I remember when I was a kid, my father asked if I wanted to go into his auto repair business with him. Even though I loved fixing cars, I said, "no." I was too young to be asked the question, and too stupid to realize I'd answered too quickly.

Thereafter, it was generally accepted that I was going to do something of a professional nature; something that would help me avoid what my parents saw as the hardship in their own lives. I didn't want to be a doctor. What I looked forward to was law school, and then going into business.

As time went by, I lost sight of the fact that I never intended to be a lawyer in the first place; that I'd gone to law school only as a means of learning how business is done. And while practicing, I fooled myself into believing that I was participating in my clients' businesses and was therefore a businessman myself.

What I've learned since is that when a client called me to do what I thought was initiating a transaction, he was really calling me to finish it. You see, to me that phone call was the beginning of the excitement. To the client, it was the end of it. He'd been pursuing the deal for a long time, and finally he had it put together. All he wanted me to do was to get it in writing and not screw it up in the process. The client didn't want to hear from me six reasons why he couldn't, or shouldn't, complete a deal. He just wanted to be told where to sign. As a lawyer, I wasn't really involved in their businesses. I only handled their legal matters. One day, I woke up and realized that I was just kidding myself if I thought that somehow I would get more involved in a business way with some of my clients.

Two things kept me tied to law for so long. First, I decided to wait until my stock interest in the firm built up to the point where leaving made good financial sense. The other tie was loyalty to my partners. I spent nearly a year wrestling with how I could both develop real estate and practice law. I wanted to structure an arrangement that my partners would find acceptable and, at the same time, give me enough latitude to pursue my real passion. What finally helped me make my break was the realization that I could not wear two hats effectively.

I like doing what I'm doing now. I'm much more satisfied with the buildings I construct than I ever was drafting a contract, no matter how brilliantly I might have conceived it. And I take pride in knowing that what I have accomplished over the last few years, I've done by sticking it out, working hard, taking the bad news and rolling with it, and staying in.

Coping Within the Law

Blessed be he who has found his work; he needs no further blessing.

◆

THOMAS CARLYLE

When a Washington, D.C. litigator told his law firm he wanted to spend more time with his family, it was suggested that he accept one of the verities of private practice: associates don't have time for conventional family life. (Or, as stated by a Los Angeles attorney, "The business of lawyering has just become too highly competitive to allow us the luxury of such personal choices.")[1] Finding that response unacceptable, the litigator resigned to become a law school professor.

For many lawyers, the profession's alluring qualities cannot be ignored. But the disadvantages continue to nag at them as well. As a consequence, they yearn for work that is less demanding or more creative; work that permits greater flexibility and more time off; work that contributes more meaningfully to society. There will always be those who merely daydream about what they think is the ultimate solution: winning the "big one" that funds a permanent retirement. But a growing number of practitioners want to have their cake and eat it too. In other words, they want to find a way to alleviate their distress without abandoning their profession, or even giving up private practice.

WORK RELEASE PROGRAMS

Alternative employment arrangements are evolving to meet the needs of those attorneys who enjoy the work, but who don't enjoy the way it tyrannizes their lives. Contract employment and part-time practice are two popular options.

The best evidence of the popularity of contract employment is the nationwide surge in contract lawyer employment agencies. These firms act as middlemen in matching law firms with qualified temporary employees. Hourly rates generally range from $18 to as much as $90, depending on geography, specialty and experience. The arrangements are beneficial to both parties: the law firm can handle fluctuations in its work load by hiring attorneys who want to work on a flexible basis, and the contract attorney can work when he or she wants and receive a fair return for every hour of labor.

Part-time permanent practice is another option, primarily selected by women with young children. These practitioners generally have worked full time (which means overtime in this business) as an associate with a firm before they request a conversion to part-time status. Usually, that translates to two-thirds to four-fifths of the normal billable hour requirement with a concomitant cut in pay. Some firms have instituted policies permitting any associate to arrange a part-time schedule for up to one year. In almost all cases, though, the associate forfeits or delays partnership consideration.

Part-time work, while less popular with men, is still a viable option. One litigation partner of a New York City law firm decided to split his time practicing law so he could also counsel attorneys about career direction. In another case, the former partner of a business litigation firm chose to work on a contract basis with his old firm to allow him the luxury of writing novels. Still another shares child-care duties with his wife by working part-time.

Julie, a part-time associate at a fast-growing West Coast law firm, researched the subject of part-time practice for a seminar in her city. "My sample may not have been scientifically accurate," she said. "But, one thing came through loud and clear: part-time lawyers are generally a lot happier than most of the full-time variety."

Robin entered the legal profession in the late 1970's determined to succeed on her own terms. After a few years with a small law firm, she hung out her own shingle to practice with a style and focus that was totally her own. In 1982, after the birth of her first child, she reduced her practice by half. Now divorced and sharing custody of her two children, *Robin* has learned what works, and what doesn't, in running a part-time practice.

◆

Robin's Profile

B.A., University of Minnesota, 1974
J.D., University of Minnesota, 1977
Associate, small general practice firm, 1977-81
Solo practitioner, 1981-82
Currently, part-time solo practitioner

Robin's Statement: With six years of experience practicing part-time, I know exactly what's necessary to do it. First, you have to cut your overhead. Second, you have to narrow your scope. Third, you have to swallow your pride.

I was prepared for my income to drop 30 percent when I switched to half time, but actually I make as much money now as I did when I was working full time. The key is keeping my overhead down. I work primarily out of my house. In order to sit down with clients occasionally, I rent a tiny office from a law firm with leftover space. For typing, I use a local entrepreneur who does freelance word processing at a very reasonable price. I keep my eye on the cost of supplies, malpractice insurance, and accounting fees.

The next requirement is to narrow your scope. I accomplished that goal at the outset by firing the clients who either didn't pay me, or who forced me to beg for a percentage on the dollar. By the time I moved my business home, I could tell on the telephone which clients were not likely to pay. They usually tipped their hand by making the same sort of remarks as the last 10 people who wound up not paying. So, I got rid of all those cases, and now I regularly turn away new business that looks like trouble. I only take cases that are interesting, with people I like and who are likely to pay me. I've

113

lowered my stress and increased my income. The time I work is time well spent.

I have a lot more control over my income by running a much tighter ship. When I worked full time, I'd have 60, 70, even 80 cases going at a time. I was occasionally out of control and always working too hard. Now, I'm down to 20 to 25 cases of different sizes, but mostly fairly small. The smaller my operation gets, the more control I have. I'm not under stress, because I weeded out most of the bad cases and I know what I'm doing.

Which leads to another element of narrowing your scope: carving out a specialty. When I started my practice, I would take the case of anyone who walked in my door. No more. General practice is too hard now, period. And if you are going to work part-time, it's ridiculous. Now, my practice is limited to guardianship and probate, a specialty that's affected by only one section of the legislative code. I don't have to worry as much about keeping up with changes in the law.

It's important to pick a specialty that avoids complex matters and high-stress litigation. The only exception I would make is a wrongful death case with no liability issues, like a father of three getting run over in a crosswalk by a well-insured driver. But how many cases like that are you likely to get? In 11 years of practice, I haven't gotten one. If you don't have the support you need, you cannot handle a complicated lawsuit against a big corporation. You have to leave that for the full-time lawyers. The case may look attractive, but if it's stressful and will require costs to be advanced, you're getting yourself right back into what you just finished leaving.

Swallowing your pride — the last requirement — means using an answering machine instead of employing a full-time receptionist or paying for an answering service. It means doing without the fancy office and the personal secretary. It means that when someone asks if they can schedule a motion on Thursday afternoon, you have to admit that your preschooler's play takes priority. Fortunately, I find other lawyers to be much more responsive to that kind of scheduling problem than they would be if my conflict involved a very important deposition in "my Union Oil case."

I found full-time law practice relentless. There was never any time to breathe. Even if I was vacationing, I was always worrying about my cases. On a part-time basis, things are not as relentless. I work about 25 hours per week. My kids are finally in school, and I have some free time. There's only one problem with this whole arrangement. If you get into good part-time work, it's difficult to imagine going back to full-time employment. But I still recommend trying part-time practice. The worst thing that can happen is that you have to go back to working full time.

SWITCHING SIDES

A seat on the bench is another attractive way to avoid many of the stresses that plague the general practitioner. Although some attorneys forsake high incomes for an appointment to the judiciary, judges still earn comfortable salaries and in most jurisdictions receive generous retirement benefits. They never have to worry about billing clients or collecting fees, nor about rising overhead. The cases judges decide have beginnings, middles and ends that generally occur over the span of a few days. And, most importantly, they exercise the power to bring closure to those conflicts.

The choice to move to the bench is not, of course, available to every practicing attorney. The lawyer must either be well-respected among those with the power to make appointments, or capable of winning an election for the seat. More significantly, judges must find enough value in the adversarial system to tolerate sitting in the middle of argument and hostility. And, they must learn to endure constant public scrutiny, second-guessing and criticism.

Judge Smith entered the profession at a time when there were few women lawyers, and female litigators were even rarer. In defense against anonymity, she resorted to wearing loud hats and eccentric clothing in court, and brandishing her advocacy like a weapon. But as her legal reputation grew, *Judge Smith* gradually relaxed and started each lawsuit in a novel fashion: by making a pact with opposing counsel to avoid mutual hostility. Eventually, though, she wearied of private practice. After four years of active lobbying, she was appointed to her current trial court position in 1984.

Judge Smith's Profile

B.A., University of Oregon, 1966
J.D., University of Idaho, 1969
General civil practice, emphasizing litigation, 1970-84
L.L.M., Taxation, New York University, 1982
Currently, trial court judge

Judge Smith's Statement: Back in 1970, the senior partner of the firm I joined said to me, "Someday you're going to be on the bench." I laughed it off because that was not what I saw for myself. I saw myself as a firebreathing litigator.

In my first four years of practice, it was my goal to do every kind of proceeding and action at least once. What I ended up enjoying most was the trial work. But as a woman lawyer in the early 1970's, I didn't have many examples to follow. At one extreme, there were women lawyers in title companies, and at the other, there was "Bernice the Bitch." By the time I was ready to go out on my own, I decided that if I had to choose one image, I'd be like Bernice, which in those days meant being pretty abrasive and strident. But, remember, back then, if a woman didn't throw down the gauntlet right away, she got run over.

I worked horrendous hours, because when men opposed me (which was almost all the time), they tended to prepare harder. They took it very personally if they lost a case to a woman, as if somehow it was a challenge to their manhood. Fortunately, as my reputation preceded me, men expected a female barracuda, and I could afford to be nicer.

As I became more experienced, the first thing I would do in almost every major case was to take the opposing counsel to lunch. I spent half the time talking about the case and the other half speaking personally, finding out whether the lawyer was married and had kids, what his hobbies were, what other pressures he might be experiencing in addition to the case we had in common, and how all these factors might affect the progress of our case. If possible, I'd make a little pact to avoid hostility between us even as we advocated the clients' hostilities.

As the years went by, though, I noticed that attorneys were becoming less and less cooperative. There was no such thing as settling a case over a cup of coffee. It was all so stress-producing that I used to come home like a helicopter setting down. I was all wired up, outraged and upset. In time, all that combat steered me into the judiciary.

I still feel the wear and tear of the adversarial system. In fact, the hardest adjustment in moving to the bench was shedding the adversarial role. As a judge, you have to sit back and wait for the other side to wage their attack. With my background as a litigator, that was difficult. I would listen to one side's arguments and force myself not to cut in and say, "Well what about this," and "What about that," and "Gee, haven't you considered this, this and this?" I had to consciously jump back from an adversarial orientation to become the decider. That's turned out to be the best thing about being a judge — the opportunity to do what I think is right. And, in some ways, it's the worst too, because it is an awesome challenge.

There are downsides to being a judge. First of all, the loneliness of the judiciary is not overrated. And I'm definitely more restricted in my public interaction, having to watch what I say about everything. I'm never sure if some inadvertent statement I make is going to end up being lambasted on the front page of the newspaper.

All in all, though, I find this very satisfying. The last four years have been the best years of my life.

SWITCHING CELLS

Most licensed attorneys find it difficult to abandon the profession without looking back. And, concerned that they give their career every consideration, they trade one job for another *within* the profession until they find the right niche. Some move from private practice to public practice or corporate counsel; others from one area of law to another, or from politics to the court system and back again. With enough exploration and persistence, many of them eventually settle into a reasonably satisfying alternative.

Tom made two mistakes in getting his legal career off the ground. First, he went to law school before he was ready to make a commitment to the profession. Then, when he finally decided to take his degree seriously, he accepted the first job he was offered without exploring whether the subject matter, or style of his employer, suited his talents and personality. As a result, *Tom* was pigeonholed for five years in an environment he did not enjoy. Only through a series of lucky breaks did he finally discover a specialty he now finds thoroughly enjoyable.

◆

Tom's Profile

B.A., University of Michigan, 1966
J.D., George Washington University, 1969
Complaint review, EEOC, 1969
Specialist on drug abuse legislation, National Institute of Mental Health, 1970-72
Part-time editor, legal publisher, 1973-77
Associate for solo practitioner, 1977-81
Associate, small intellectual property firm, 1981-87
Currently, solo practitioner

Tom's Statement: I went to law school without any expectation of ever practicing… I just wanted to stay out of the Army. Once I accomplished that, I didn't take my career seriously until almost 10 years later.

When I got married in 1977, I approached a solo practitioner for a job as an associate. I walked in, said, "Here I am," and he said, "Okay. You're hired." The next four years consisted of a series of emergencies. It was Band Aid law; I was always patching up this guy's mistakes. I learned a little bit about all of his work, mostly personal injury lawsuits with some real estate, probate, and misdemeanors thrown in. But I never felt comfortable with any of it.

Once, for a few months, I quit to write science fiction, and for the first time in years I felt I was doing the right thing. But, then we needed money and I didn't know how else to earn it. So, I went back to work for him again. By the time I left for good, I had two children and didn't see fiction writing as a viable option to support them. Instead, I advertised in the legal newspapers for work assignments from other attorneys, set up an office in my home and waited for the calls to come in.

Rather than generating freelance work, the advertisement led to my next job. A three-person firm handling a huge patent case was facing three firms on the other side and was dying for help. I joined them on a provisional basis (writing responses to summary judgment motions). They liked my work so well that I was asked to join the firm.

That was where law opened up for me. Here was a whole new area to explore — patents, copyrights, trademarks — and I was pleasantly surprised to discover how well it suited my style. The litigation moved more slowly. Writing was very important; often, cases were won on the briefs I produced. I worked for six years as part of that firm, until they dissolved in April, 1987. Now I do the same kind of work as an independent contractor for one of them, but the bulk of my practice is with my *own* clients. I emphasize "own," because this is where the satisfaction comes from: making the decisions, being the one in charge, taking the risks and reaping the rewards myself.

I still consider getting out of law every once in a while. The last time was about a year ago, when we were in the middle of a big trade secrets lawsuit. The case took on a terribly combative tone, and it drove me crazy. At first, it was horrible waking up Monday morning. Pretty soon, I contracted "Sunday Syndrome," dreading Monday when I awoke on Sunday. Eventually, the only good time of the week was Friday night because I still had all day Saturday before I felt that dread of heading back to the office again.

Other lawyers might crave winning; speaking the loudest and the most quickly to get the judge to believe them. But that's not for me. I've set limits now on my practice. When I accept a big litigation case, I associate a trial counsel to handle the things I don't like, leaving me to do what I enjoy most: the client contact, research, motion and appeals practice, being the lead counsel. My practice is gently adversarial and scholarly, and I no longer feel any pressing urge to leave. Still, when things get rough, my fantasies take me to the woods of Mendocino, where I'm dressed in blue jeans and a corduroy shirt... and I'm writing novels.

FURLOUGHS

As the pressures of practicing law increase, more attorneys are looking for ways to take long breaks from their work. Nationwide, many law firms have instituted sabbatical policies allowing partners (not associates) three to six months off every four to six years with no cut in salary. In a few firms, sabbaticals are even required in an effort to prevent burnout. But in most, these extended vacations are options taken by only a small percentage of those who qualify.[2]

Even solo practitioners, and those from small firms, can take advantage of sabbaticals. One busy graduate from the University of California at Davis took two six-month sabbaticals in seven years, each time closing her office and reopening it in a new location, with a different clientele. Her secret? Conscientiously saving money, believing in her ability to start over again, and getting fed up enough to risk it all.

Jon is a top-rate litigation partner who handles the most complex and crucial of his firm's court cases. While the glamor and challenge of being in the courtroom excite him, trial work these days mostly occurs in his or some other lawyer's offices. In 1980, while still an associate at the firm, *Jon* took a three-month unpaid sabbatical. Later, when he qualified for a paid sabbatical, he again left the country.

What does the respite do for busy practitioners? What attitudes do they bring back with them to work? Although the answers are as varied as the people who take sabbaticals, *Jon* represents those who believe that a three- to six-month respite merely pacifies, but does not permanently erase, a growing dissatisfaction with the profession.

◆

Jon's Profile
B.A., Williams College, 1970
J.D., Columbia Law School, 1974
Assistant U.S. attorney, 1974-76
Currently, litigation partner, corporate law firm

Jon's Statement: Both of my sabbaticals lasted three months. In 1986, I traveled through the South Pacific. In 1980, I traveled through

120

Asia, and it really gave me a different perspective on life. When you go somewhere like Bombay, India, and see people in loincloths sleeping in the streets, or living in little cardboard shacks, you come back thinking your problems aren't quite so big.

I took my watch off the day that I left on sabbatical, and didn't put it on until the day I came back. There was no worrying about billable hours, or accounts receivable, or getting clients. The big issues in life became, "What am I going to eat today?" and "What am I going to do?" I ate when I was hungry; slept when I was tired. For me, high stress was missing a plane.

On a sabbatical, you aren't judged. No one figures out who you are by what you do. You're just another traveler. You don't have 25 phone messages to return that day. You don't have all these hassles of deadlines and clients and judges and other lawyers on your ass. You're not constantly competing. You're not always trying to achieve something; to maintain some prescribed level of success.

In my experience, though, the effects of each sabbatical lasted little more than two months. After a short while — this happened to me each time — I'd be back on a fast track for trial, getting tense and biting my fingernails; in the middle of the same old scene. Last year, after the second sabbatical, I had four trials from April to December and ended up working our law firm hourly average, even though I was only there about eight months of the year. I was the first person in the firm to get a bonus in the year of my sabbatical because I put in so many hours.

In the long run, I'm not sure sabbaticals do anything for you, other than create great anticipation for the next one. Three months off might seem like a lot of time to some people. But let me tell you, it's not long enough to make you seriously think about getting out. Half way through both sabbaticals, I remember thinking, "Gee, it's half gone and pretty soon I have to go back." Then, before I knew it, the end was only two or three weeks away and I was disappointed and sad that it was all coming to a close. In terms of long-range career implications, I don't think my sabbaticals were of any benefit to me.

Taking a longer sabbatical might be more helpful, or even spending three months by myself in a cabin in the woods. It might give me more time to think about what I really want to do; whether I should be practicing law at all, or practicing a different kind of law, or in a different environment.

We used to have a deal where you could skip sabbaticals and double up; instead of taking one every three years, you could take six months every six years. About two years ago, for economic reasons alone, the partners not only barred doubling up, but extended the time in between sabbaticals from three years to four. I won't qualify again until 1992 and that's a long way off. Even though I'm skeptical about the lasting benefits of sabbaticals, I still would rather make a lot less money and have a lot more time off.

RECIDIVISM

In their book, *The Addictive Organization*, Ann Wilson Schaef and Dianne Fasel contend that "anything can be addictive when it becomes so central to a person that life feels impossible without it."[3] In that sense, being a lawyer and belonging to the legal system can be powerful addictions, leading to a pattern that mimics that of other substance abusers. Some attorneys who fit this profile drop out for a year or two when their lives seem completely out of control and they can't stand being in the profession another minute. As soon as they recover some balance, however, too many of them relapse by diving back into the grip of their familiar addiction.

What often breaks this demoralizing cycle is taking time out for introspection. With the help of career counselors, psychotherapists, 12-step programs, or even personal growth seminars, attorneys can begin to uncover the issues undermining their respect for the profession and their willingness to participate in it. In time, they can discard old work habits and attitudes, and learn how to practice law in a way which nurtures their emotional health. Lawyers who make constructive changes within themselves, as well as in their outlook on life, are then able to resume their practices with a greater sense of resolve.

In 1979, *Phil* escaped from law for the glamor of facilitating transformational seminars. During his three years away, he came to realize that he himself was the source of his professional dissatisfaction.

With fresh insight, *Phil* returned, a decision that has resulted in a partnership interest in a corporate litigation firm and greatly increased job satisfaction.

◆

Phil's Profile

U.S. Army, 1966-70
B.A., University of Arizona, 1973
J.D., University of Arizona, 1976
Associate, insurance defense and corporate law firm, 1976-79
Facilitator, personal effectiveness training seminar, 1979-81
Currently, partner in corporate law firm

Phil's Statement: In 1979, I was a fourth-year associate in a small trial firm. I worked on a number of large-scale, complex and esoteric cases. I was getting good results. I was liked by the partners and advancing rather quickly. But, basically, I was bored.

I'm sure I had expressed some dissatisfaction with law before then, but I didn't express any moral reservations about it until after I participated in a series of transformational workshops. I took a rather strong stance that the legal system was all screwed up, and that the adversarial process, where people try to beat each other's brains out to get resolution, was stupid and couldn't work. I saw each of my cases as situations in which my client was somewhat responsible for creating the problem. But rather than trying to resolve it, my client wanted to blame somebody else. And he was so chicken about it that he had to pay a lawyer to do it for him. Telling myself that it was all inconsistent with my values gave me an excuse to do something different. With that background, I accepted a job offer to facilitate personal growth seminars in San Francisco.

When I announced that I was leaving the firm, the partners responded by telling me that they were prepared — right then — to offer me a shareholder position. I gulped and thought, "Gee, I'm giving up some equity here. Is this really what I want to do?" Other than that moment, though, I had no second thoughts about my decision to leave. I was excited to death to be getting away from law.

123

I packed up the family and moved to San Francisco. The first seminar I led was sometime in the summer of 1980. Later that year, I decided I was in love with one of the other seminar facilitators. So, my wife and I split up, and I remarried and moved to Portland, Oregon. Shortly after we arrived, a philosophical difference over the management of the seminar company caused both of us to resign from our positions.

There we were in a new city, both of us unemployed. I had a new family, as well as a child support commitment. I needed to find something to do, but I had real difficulty in the job market. Every time I'd go in for an interview in sales or management, I'd be asked, "What are you doing in this office? You're a lawyer." I'd start to explain and watch the interviewer's eyes glaze over. So, after a couple of months of dead ends, I registered for the Oregon bar examination.

Even though, just a few months earlier, I had been resistant to going back to the law, I felt committed to taking the bar exam. I didn't give much thought to the value conflict I agonized over years before. I just wanted to be gainfully employed, and this was the safest thing I could do. It was, in fact, my only real choice.

For the most part, practicing law has been fun since I returned. This firm has quadrupled since I joined. I'm a partner now. There's a feeling of excitement in the air. Even so, from time to time, I get some of the same feelings I had in the past. There are times when I get bored; when I don't want to come into the office. But whenever I start thinking, "Is this what I want to be doing every day?," I remember that twice now I've worked toward building something and left just as the pay-off was about to occur. Now, I'm ready to see one through.

What's different is that after leading transformational programs for two years, I view the law and the legal profession in a new context. I recognize that my actions have a lot to do with creating an atmosphere of compromise. If I bait the other side with a "Your-client-is-a-stupid-shit-and-we're-going-to-knock-your-brains-out-in-court," I'm going to get that back. If I take a reasonable approach, the other lawyer will too.

It doesn't work for me to get down on, or upset with, other lawyers. Lawyers are just people, and most of them are pretty nice people who sometimes forget that they don't have to be difficult. If you remind them, like any human being, they go, "Phew. Thank goodness." They really do.

I am not on a crusade to change the way we practice law. Saying we should have a system that works differently is really saying that people should be different. That's ridiculous; people are the way they are. Some clients will want to work things out. The majority of the population isn't that way, nor would they be even if all of the lawyers were removed from the world.

I believe that some system as an alternative to violence is necessary to resolve conflict between human beings. And certainly, the problems of the current system are not going to go away if lawyers leave when they decide the adversarial system is defective. Instead, people with that kind of consciousness should stay in the system and encourage their clients to deal responsibly with their problems.

Rehabilitating the System

Whatever you can do or dream you can, begin it.
Boldness has genius, power and magic in it.

♦

GOETHE

"The problems of the current system," said *Phil*, "are not going to go away if lawyers leave when they decide the adversarial system is defective." And yet, that's precisely the choice that more and more good lawyers are considering these days.

As a whole, those who *do* leave the law — whether they're walking or running — have resigned themselves to the status quo. "It's too big of a problem to become a crusader," shrugged *Kate* in Chapter 3. "After all, I'm not Mother Teresa." Or, as *Bo* said in Chapter 5, "If the legal system could be rehabilitated over the next 10 or 15 years, that would be a challenge worth accepting. But I don't think the practice of law is going to change. And, if it can't be rehabilitated, I'm not going to stick around and get battered trying to fix it."

Even if they've given up on the legal system, though, these professional emigrants still seem intent on making a contribution to society. In fact, most are searching for environments in which they feel they can play a more meaningful role. "What I want to do now is something that has a positive effect on the way people live," said *Michael* in Chapter 3. And that desire extends to their participation in their own families. "We've only got our kids for X number of years," concluded *Earl* in Chapter 3, "and then it's all over. What we do as lawyers is frivolous compared to that."

But even as more lawyers are leaving, or at least giving the idea more serious thought than ever before, the professional establishment won't acknowledge that anything is very seriously wrong! Their own surveys report that almost a fifth of all lawyers are unhappy with their employment and that nearly half would not again choose law as a career. But the American Bar Association wonders whether this "seeming groundswell" of dissatisfaction is really an accurate picture of the profession.[1] What makes the situation even more intolerable is that the longer attorneys practice and the more satisfied they become, the more influence they tend to have over the operation of law firms, courts and bar associations. In other words, practitioners who have the greatest investment in the status quo are the very lawyers most likely to hold the reins.

According to Schaef and Fasel in *The Addictive Organization*, a closed system which uses denial as its major defense mechanism, will "lose its best people" if it continues to operate in that dysfunctional fashion.[2] It could be argued that lawyers who do leave the profession are only behaving naturally in an uncomfortable situation. But from another point of view, they are just as culpable as their former peers in maintaining the current state of affairs. "The legal system will be awful forever," said *Mary Kay*, featured in Chapter 5, "if everyone who thinks it's awful will have nothing to do with it."

Between attitudes of resignation and complacency, *the legal profession does seem destined to perpetuate its problems*: the hourly billing "rat race" that is the economic foundation of law; the deterioration of interpersonal relationships among lawyers; and the overly adversarial and clinical nature of the lawyer's role in modern times. The irony is that even these highly complex problems are curable by making only two simple attitudinal shifts.

The first is acknowledging that the current level of lawyer disaffection negatively impacts the well-being of the entire profession.

The second is accepting responsibility to make things better.

FIRST AREA OF IMPROVEMENT: THE ECONOMICS OF LAW

Reliance upon the hourly billing system continues to trap practitioners in a no-win cycle. Clients naturally want their problems handled as quickly and cheaply as possible, but many lawyers are rewarded solely on the basis of the time they spend pursuing a solution. Billing by the hour, therefore, places the client's and the attorney's interests in direct conflict. Moreover, because lawyers are selling time, as *Bradley* stated in Chapter 3, they often succumb to the "temptation to spend all of it practicing law." With the forces of inflation and competition making it even harder to earn a living, that "temptation" is now a necessity. "If lawyers want to stop working like wage-hour slaves," *Bradley* continued, "they have to get past their risk-averse mentality" to experiment with other fee systems.

In 1956, George D. Hornstein wrote in the *Harvard Law Review* that, "A surgeon who performs an appendectomy in seven minutes is entitled to no smaller fee than one who takes an hour; many a patient would think [the doctor] is entitled to more." Similarly, an attorney who resolves a potentially expensive conflict in a 15-minute telephone call should be entitled to substantially more compensation than a fourth of his hourly rate, especially when a more combative or less experienced attorney might charge hundreds of thousands of dollars for the same result. With that reasoning in mind, the American Bar Association's Section on Legal Economics is now studying the application of Hornstein's theory, and other forms of "value billing," as possible solutions to the financial difficulties of the profession.

Obviously, the hardest part of implementing a value billing system is figuring out a fair way to price the infinite number of legal services offered to the public. But despite the difficulties, the profession's long-term survival calls for creative alternatives to the mere recording of, and charging for, all the time spent on a client's matter. This could entail any one of a number of options:

- Setting standard prices for routine work.
- Negotiating flat fee agreements which outline the approach the attorney will take, and what cooperation is required of the client.
- Charging by the hour with a bonus paid for results which are accomplished within a certain time frame, or which avoid litigation.
- Tying fees to the recovery received by the client, but reducing the attorney's reward on a per hour basis the longer it takes to secure it.

Any one of these proposals would result in a system that compensates lawyers, again in *Bradley*'s words, for their "thoughtful, mature, experienced judgment," and not for contentious, aggressive or inefficient actions. The more quickly, smoothly and painlessly an attorney could resolve a conflict or a deal, the happier the client would be and the better the lawyer would be rewarded for his time. As one current practitioner put it, "Our profession will gain credibility and, to some extent, get back in the good graces of the public if we look at fairness first and time expended later."[3] But the suggested modifications to the billing system would only succeed in a changed working environment: one focused on problem solving instead of winning; one that operates with mutual respect and courtesy.

SECOND AREA OF IMPROVEMENT: COLLEGIALITY

As *Cindy* complained in Chapter 4, "The law firm system doesn't make any sense. Associates get lots of financial perks, but when it comes to nurturing job satisfaction, the partners have no interest." As a result, more than half of all law school graduates who enter private practice resign from their first job within four years. The firms' typical response further aggravates the situation. Rather than explore why associates leave, and perhaps ameliorate employment conditions, they simply pressure the remaining associates to bill more hours and become more profitable to make up for the wasted expense of recruitment and training, and the fees paid to legal search consultants. In this way, a vicious cycle develops. As associates watch their peers being courted by competing firms, they wonder why they continue to endure the treatment that drove the others away, and they themselves seek out headhunters. Thus, by denying that a problem exists, the firms lose their "best people" — the bright, young associates they so earnestly courted.

Law firms could be more sensitive to the special needs of the members of their professional staffs. Lawyer and management consultant Richard Feferman says that law firms should "strive to treat everyone fairly — instead of treating them all alike."[4] Associates frequently complain that the only reinforcement they receive for a job well done is a standardized annual raise. But once lawyers reach a comfortable income level (which, for some, is their starting salary), added dollars often fail to be motivators. Law firms need to evaluate, on a case-by-case basis, what will provide adequate reward and encouragement to the members of the firm. For example, offering more time off to an associate with a young family might mean more than a five percent increase in salary. Others may want more time in the limelight, more autonomy, or simply more praise. What law firm managers need to keep in mind is that lawyers are not inventory; they're human beings with varying responses to life.

Firms could trade their hierarchical structure for something more democratic. For example, every attorney enters as a partner in the Manhattan law firm of Anderson, Russel, Kill & Olick, and takes part in determining compensation levels of everyone else. The firm runs according to "Twelve Principles" established by founder Eugene Anderson; principles which emphasize community service and a high level of personal satisfaction over maximizing earnings. Although the firm's senior partners are well paid, they have consciously forfeited the sort of skyrocketing compensation of other lawyers in town who earn their high incomes off the sweat and dissatisfaction of their subordinates. As a direct result, the firm experiences very little turnover in manpower. Says one young member, "This place really takes a lot of the agony out of the profession."[5]

Law firms ought to encourage open communication among partners and associates. As an example, in the New York firm of Kramer, Levin, Nesen, Kamin & Frankel, associates are asked to evaluate — anonymously — the behavior of the partners. At an annual retreat, the often "scathingly brutal" critiques are reviewed with the assistance of psychiatrist Samuel C. Klagsbrun, who has worked with the firm for two decades. According to Dr. Klagsbrun, the annual review process is highly cathartic, and crucial to the healthy operation of the firm.[6]

Bar associations and law firms ought to establish employee assistance programs. Several bar associations have already founded such programs as a means of averting potential disciplinary actions. They guarantee confidentiality and respond to both third-party complaints and self-referred practitioners who are experiencing problems with depression, alcoholism or other substance abuse. Few law firms, however, have adopted the corporate trend of providing employee assistance programs (EAP's). In an EAP, trained counselors — either working in-house or operating according to a contract with the firm — offer limited counseling, and if further assistance is needed, refer the troubled employee to an outside professional. Firms without the revenue to support a full-blown EAP could consider adding to their compensation packages such benefits as insurance coverage for psychological counseling, contribution toward career counseling, or tuition for aptitude testing or personal effectiveness training.

THIRD AREA OF IMPROVEMENT: LEGAL EDUCATION

According to one study, "professional schools are highly invasive institutions which exert intense control by purposely influencing beliefs, values and personality characteristics of students; and law schools appear to be the most invasive among all graduate education."[7] The traditional law school curriculum trains students "for combat rather than the gentler arts of reconciliation and accommodation."[8] And faculties justify the retention of this approach by insisting that their task is to teach the law's specialized logic and critical analysis, not the practical applications of those theories. But that thinking denies the reality of the extraordinary power that law schools wield to shape the entire legal profession. Another area of critical reform, therefore, is legal education.

Law schools ought to provide comprehensive career planning. Most accredited law schools run placement offices which cater to the recruitment needs of large law firms. Some also offer workshops which outline the range of opportunities available to law school graduates in law and law-related fields. A few schools have career and/or psychological counselors available to help students with their decision-making. But a more complete program, one which provides a realistic look at the everyday practice of law as well as assistance with career evaluation and planning, would help students identify *appropriate* career options, and encourage them to enter post-graduate fields that more closely suit their temperaments and complement their values.

Law schools ought to require a general liberal arts education. Today's pre-law students often avoid coursework in philosophy, psychology or English literature in favor of economics and business accounting classes. "They prepare themselves to justify the money that they expect to earn," says District of Columbia practitioner Sol Linowitz. "We don't give them the encouragement to become broad-based people." Linowitz proposes that law students be required to take one course in the humanities during each year of law school. "You can often learn more about people from great novels than you can from studying the law books," he says.[9]

Law schools ought to emphasize conciliation, diplomacy and effective interpersonal skills rather than pure advocacy. The curriculum would more positively contribute to the profession if it were expanded beyond the theoretical and into the practical aspects of law practice — fact-finding, interviewing, inspiring confidence, negotiating, understanding other's viewpoints, and building relationships that work. Law students could use more practical training in interpersonal skills, perhaps being required to take courses in counseling or human behavior. Since an understanding of human motivations, professional etiquette and ethics are so closely intertwined, adding people-centered coursework to the intellectual focus of law school would undoubtedly set a tone of fair play among graduates.

FOURTH AREA OF IMPROVEMENT: CIVILITY

No matter what law schools emphasize, if graduates enter practice and discover that a courteous and conciliatory style (especially in litigation) puts them at a strategic disadvantage, and earns no offsetting rewards from their employers, they'll choose to be more combative. And that's certainly the message the profession has been sending. Hiring partners make it clear that they seek those, as described by *Linda* in Chapter 3, who are "smarter, faster, and more predatory." Job applicants to some law firms have reported that they forfeited their opportunity for employment by revealing a commitment to mediation. This thinking couldn't be more wrong-headed, and calls for a joint effort by the powers of the legal community.

Senior lawyers should take the lead in improving the quality of professional activity. At the American Bar Association's 1988 annual meeting, the Commission on Professionalism asked partners to evaluate the message they send to their professional staffs as role models of ethical standards and professional decorum. For example:

- Are clients invited to critique the interpersonal skills of the firm's attorneys, as well as the quality of the legal work?
- When partners review associates' overall annual performance, do they concentrate on service to the client and the profession over billable hours and loyalty to the firm?
- Have the partners implemented in-house training sessions, perhaps using role playing, in the areas of the etiquette of negotiation, responses to contentious behavior by opposing counsel, and the control of vengeful clients? (One California firm, for example, discovered a surprising trend in a mock negotiation session attended by all of their associates. Many of the participants exhibited such tactics as withholding evidence or shading the facts, which were on the "margin" of ethics.)[10]

Law firms could also consider the adoption of the ABA model credo, which states, "I will advise my client that civility and courtesy are not to be equated with weakness," and "I will endeavor to be courteous and civil, both in oral and in written communications." Adopting a creed without living it, however, will impress no one. "The only way lawyers are going to change their image is by their daily conduct," says Sam Dash, professor at Georgetown University Law Center. "If you're a professional, you don't need a Boy Scout oath. If you're not a professional, a Boy Scout oath is a flim-flam."[11]

Bar associations ought to require members to attend seminars and workshops on "professionalism" in order to maintain their licenses to practice. Many jurisdictions have already institutionalized mandatory legal education programs, but the choice of coursework falls totally within the discretion of the individual practitioner. Bar associations could contribute greatly to a more civilized working environment by requiring members to study, in a formal setting, issues of common courtesy and cooperation. At a minimum, articles such as the *ABA Journal*'s "Rambo Litigation — Why Hardball Tactics Don't Work"[12] and books such as *GETTING TO YES: Negotiating Agreements Without Giving In,*"[13] ought to be required reading for all practicing lawyers. Better yet, associations could mandate attendance at a wide variety of seminars, ranging from such topics as diplomatic negotiation to human behavior, from the mechanics of good communication to ethical dilemmas.

Organizations of lawyers ought to establish consultation groups. These groups would be available to all practitioners on an as-needed basis to discuss such difficulties as personality clashes, ethical questions, confusion in interpreting court rules, or coming up with a persuasive but conciliatory settlement strategy. As an alternative, names of lawyers willing to give telephone advice on issues of "professionalism" could be circulated to all association members.

FIFTH AREA OF IMPROVEMENT: EMPHASIS ON MEDIATION

In the traditional adversarial approach, lawyers concentrate first on defining the differences between their clients. Then, by touting the strength of their positions, they work toward an agreement which rewards the party in the right and penalizes the party in the wrong. The entire "discovery" process in litigation — interrogatories, depositions, motions and "give 'em the warehouse" record searches — seeks for the most part to delineate the boundaries between the parties. And, as Federal District Court Judge William Dwyer says, lawyers "have traditionally looked at settlement as something that comes along somewhere during the fight — often near the end of it — with a loss of face or a lessening of one's machismo, after a tremendous amount of money has been spent and a lot of emotional energy invested."

But Judge Dwyer applauds the emergence of a new interpretation of the trial lawyer's role in dispute resolution. "We are approaching a revised view of litigation," he says, "in which the parties can come to court looking forward not just to vindication of their rights, and not just to the traditional battle, but also to the benefit of active, positive, highly-skilled help in reaching an agreement."[14] Mediation is the primary and most popular expression of this new attitude toward conflict resolution.

Unlike litigation, where the primary goal is winning, the sole purpose of mediation is to create accord. To reach that end, each party's needs are clearly stated and sincerely considered. Then, through a process of give-and-take, everyone involved — attorneys, clients and the mediator — participates in designing an agreement that closes the deal or ends the conflict. Mediation transforms the negative approach of litigation ("Watch out!" "Don't you dare!" "Stop it!") into positive action ("Let's find something on which we can agree." "We'll do it!" "I'll help you.").

Bar associations ought to promote alternative methods of conflict resolution, including mediation. The legal establishment currently supports ADR (Alternative Dispute Resolution) primarily as a means to an end: either to lessen the court's backlog of unresolved lawsuits, or to remove from the court system altogether matters involving small amounts of money or more emotional issues (such as child custody and visitation). Bar associations could more constructively participate in the promotion of ADR by supporting it as an option to earn a living, not as a volunteer endeavor for the benefit of the court system. They could lobby their local courts to spend more money on mediation rather than on additional judges and courtrooms. And funds that are currently targeted to improving the public's perception of lawyers could be spent educating the public about the value of ADR.

Law firms could get on the mediation bandwagon. These days, business clients are demanding creative alternatives to work out their conflicts more quickly and less expensively. Law firms can either provide the service or watch their revenues decrease further. Rather than fight against the encroachment of mediation on their territory, law firms ought to diversify by opening mediation subsidiaries, or by developing in-house mediation departments to handle referrals from other law firms.

Courts ought to require evidence of good faith settlement efforts between disputants before a lawsuit can be filed. As *Phil* discussed in Chapter 8, "I saw each of my cases as situations in which my client was somewhat responsible for creating the problem. Rather than trying to resolve it, my client usually wanted to blame somebody. And he was so chicken about it that he had to pay a lawyer to do it for him." Often, lawsuits are filed out of a fear of communicating directly with the other side. In some jurisdictions, and for some types of cases, litigants are already required to enter into mediation before they can get in line for a trial date. But by making a face-to-face discussion between disputants a *pre-filing* requirement (except in emergency situations or disputes involving domestic or other violence), the backlog of court cases would soon be reduced. And, as *Linda* suggested in Chapter 3, if disputants sat down across the table from each other, in arenas in which the "duke-it-out" attorney would feel out of place, "a lot of people would go away with solutions and retain a better feeling about the whole process."

Individual lawyers ought to educate the public about non-adversar-ial approaches to conflict resolution. For the most part, attorneys accept that the courtroom should be a place of last resort to resolve conflicts. Much of the general public, however, still believes that it's the only place they'll ever find justice. That gap in enlightenment needs to be filled. As Arnold Patent suggests, lawyers ought to help their clients develop the tools to confront and resolve their own problems. In this way, preventive legal work would eventually become the lawyer's main function in society, and many of the excellent practitioners who are currently on the fence about their commitment to the profession might choose to stay.

Individual lawyers ought to take it upon themselves to represent their clients' higher purposes. "Lawyers should be more than just technicians;

137

more than tools of their clients," said *Kate* in Chapter 3. "They should be bigger than the people they're serving, using their wisdom, and some human understanding, to help people. But so many lawyers don't seem to feel they have a duty to tell the client that he's wrong." The greatest irony of the legal profession is that while lawyers often behave like hired guns, they do so because that's what their clients want. On the other hand, clients come in asking for hired guns mostly because, in their minds, that's what the profession is all about. Lawyers *could* be much more forceful about helping their clients become realistic about the problems they're facing. They could make recommendations that would minimize emotional trauma and restore peace of mind, rather than concentrating on dollars and cents, and right and wrong. They could encourage their clients to express their feelings, rather than channeling them into courtroom battles and unnecessary combativeness. And, most importantly, lawyers could separate their own agendas (such as an overdeveloped need to win or to best another lawyer) from the best interests of their clients. By appealing to their clients' highest instincts, lawyers could do plenty to change the image of the profession from a boxing ring into a peace table.

SIXTH AREA OF IMPROVEMENT: PUBLIC AWARENESS

What clients need to pay attention to, is the likelihood of being overcharged and/or underserved by the legal profession as a whole. When law firms have to absorb a small fortune in wasted law school recruitment and associate training costs, they respond by passing on at least part of the expense to their clients. When the legal profession is infected with a contentious and disagreeable mentality, consumers end up paying the cost, whether out-of-pocket or in emotional wear-and-tear.

Consumers ought to demand problem-solvers rather than zealous advocates. Better yet, they should hire lawyers who emphasize mediation and conciliation over litigation. Lawyers will, for the most part, be responsive to their clients' demands. They will do mean, nasty things in the name of the law, if that's the approach their clients want. Or, they can help their clients through difficult times with grace and compassion. The key is for consumers to shun attorneys with reputations for "taking the other side to the cleaners" or being hired guns. They should instead seek practitioners who act forcefully, but who maintain the respect and fair play so essential to continued good relationships.

Consumers ought to be full partners in the progress of their legal actions. This means clients themselves need to accept responsibility both for their part in creating whatever conflict has brought them into the legal system, and for guiding their legal representatives toward solution. It also helps if they:

- Seek peace of mind rather than a windfall or revenge.
- Are completely truthful and make a full disclosure to their attorneys.
- Are willing to listen to reason.
- Ask for and heed advice that will bring quick closure to the problem.
- Are realistic about both the economic and emotional costs of protracted litigation.
- Play an active, but not meddling, role in deciding case strategy.
- Let go of the notion that they will find justice only in court.
- Sit down with the other side to settle the case.
- Compromise.

IN SUMMATION

The motivation to run from the law has not developed in a vacuum. Those who leave, and the ones likely to follow, are reacting to the increasingly inhospitable climate of today's legal profession. In the recent past, the establishment's denial that significant dissatisfaction existed got in the way of meaningful reforms. But that reaction can no longer be justified. And, the time has also passed for reliance upon the profession's traditional method of problem solving — interminable study and discussion. "Talking about it, arguing in court, filing papers won't change it," says ex-practitioner Ralph Warner. "Only *doing* it will change it."

The suggestions made in this chapter and elsewhere are only tokens of what can be done to create a more humane and inviting work environment, and stem the rising tide of disillusionment and disaffection among our nation's practitioners. With creativity — unshackled by precedent, unlimited by risk aversion — and a commitment to action, lawyers can, as ABA President Robert D. Raven says, "shape a better future."[15]

EPILOGUE
1991 Update

At the time *Running From the Law* was first published, I knew intuitively—but couldn't back up the feeling with any statistics—that the tide of dissatisfaction among lawyers was far from its ebb. In August 1990, I got my proof in the form of a new American Bar Association survey. As compared to results in 1984, the 1990 survey found:

- the number of dissatisfied lawyers increased by more than 25 percent;
- the number of lawyers claiming to be very satisfied with their current positions decreased 20 percent to only a third of the total, and
- dissatisfaction among in-house corporate counsel jumped 77 percent.

Finally, the percentage of those who *admitted* drinking more than six alcoholic beverages a day increased from less that one-half percent in 1984 to 13 percent six years later (this versus one percent of the general population). Even more disturbing, the level of serious alcohol consumption was greater among women lawyers (20 percent) than men (11 percent). And, four out of every five practitioners, a 291 percent increase since 1984, reported drinking something alcoholic every day of the year.

The ABA simply concluded, "Never have so many who earn so much been so unhappy."

Incongruously, even though more lawyers were less satisfied with practicing law, the number planning to change professions decreased by half. The reason? The tie of "golden handcuffs," coupled with a new and disturbing reality in the legal profession—economic insecurity. For the first time in a decade, according to the *Wall Street Journal,* "layoffs in the legal world have become commonplace."

Growing disillusionment has also spread to the next generation of practitioners. While law school applications continue to climb, most law firms have substantially reduced their recruiting efforts. In fact, during the Fall 1990 recruiting session, up to half of the confirmed law firm participants cancelled their interview sessions. In sum, law students now find themselves chasing fewer jobs in an exceptionally crowded and competitive professional environment where self-destructive behavior is fast becoming the norm.

Fortunately, more options for assistance have accompanied this rise in dissatisfaction among lawyers and law students. Growth continues in educational support groups for lawyers in transition, career counseling targeted to lawyers, and seminars and workshops on topics of interest to disillusioned practitioners. For further information about career counselors or special programs for lawyers in your geographic area, and a new 120-page manual entitled *What Can You Do with a Law Degree?: Job Options and Career Strategies for Lawyers,* please mail a self-addressed stamped envelope to Deborah L. Arron, P.O. Box 99477, Seattle, WA 98199 or telephone (206) 285-5239.

> Deborah L. Arron
> Seattle, Washington
> January 1991

APPENDICES

Appendix One:
Career Planning Tips for Dissatisfied Lawyers

THE EVALUATION PROCESS

- Take steps to raise your level of self-esteem and self-confidence.
- Talk about your dissatisfaction with other lawyers.
- Analyze and improve, if necessary, your financial condition.
- Take time off to introspect.
- Get in touch with activities you have enjoyed in the past.
- Realistically evaluate your skills.
- Stop delaying gratification.
- Don't put off decisions until you lose your job or get burned out.
- Let go of the notion that you owe a lifetime commitment to your current employer or partners, or even to your legal career.

Take steps to raise your level of self-esteem and self-confidence. One of the keys to a successful job or career change is believing that it *is* possible. This is especially true for those who seem wedded to the legal profession. Charles Prugh, a San Francisco outplacement counselor, contends that only those who are "able and willing to give up their current notion of what they are, and how they want the world to see them" will sever their ties with the profession. Says Prugh, "I know clients are ready to make a move when I hear them tell me, 'I know people see me as an attorney, but I don't give a damn now.' Until they've said good-bye to what and where they are, they won't be able to see anyplace else they can go."

If that clarity *is* absent, you need to confront your unhappiness directly. Just as you counsel others to seek professional advice in the law, you are well-advised to seek out the help of a psychologist, psychiatrist, or other trained counselor. Any assistance in this area will be helpful, and that includes group therapy, self-help books, personal effectiveness or transformational seminars, or religious or spiritual instruction. Former career counselor for lawyers Ava Butler believes, "Those who feel comfortable with who they are and where they are going are the ones who have the most success in making a job change."

Talk about your dissatisfaction with other lawyers. Many lawyers share your unhappiness, and would be relieved to know that they are not alone. Confide in a colleague you find trustworthy. That attorney may share your feelings or know of others who do. Make a point of speaking with lawyers who have recently changed jobs either in or outside of the profession. Consider starting or joining a Lawyers in Transition program (see the suggestions in the Epilogue and the next appendix). Don't isolate yourself. You do not have to feel alone.

Analyze and improve, if necessary, your financial condition. One of the first questions one career counselor puts to her lawyer clients is how much money they think they need to live. If they don't know, she instructs them to write a budget. If married, she also suggests a discussion with their spouse about what expenses they can reduce or eliminate... and still be on speaking terms.

Taking a hard line with finances is critical. You need to ask yourself how much money you are willing to risk, and what sacrifices you are willing to make, for more satisfying employment. For example, one successful practitioner had accumulated nearly $100,000 in relatively liquid investments at the time she was contemplating a career change. Although she had thought of that money as her retirement security, she decided instead to invest half of it in her own career satisfaction. By altering her lifestyle (cutting out such luxuries as meals out, expensive entertainment, manicures, and frequent travel), she stretched her funds to cover nearly two years of evaluation and introspection, and a year beyond that in the development of an entrepreneurial venture.

Take time to introspect. Spend an hour a day looking quietly inward — examining your values, your fulfillment. Better yet, go on a weekend retreat, or take an extended vacation or sabbatical, devoted solely to introspection. One theory holds that fulfillment in four areas — work, relationships, leisure and challenge — is essential to each person's sense of satisfaction. Naturally, it's unreasonable to expect your job to satisfy all four elements. So, first figure out how you meet your needs in three of the areas, and then evaluate your job. Answer questions such as these: what is most important to me? What gives me satisfaction? If I could change anything in the world, what would it be? What was I doing at those times in my life when I felt most fulfilled? How has my standard of success changed since law school? (For example, material reward or recognition as an expert might have previously motivated you, but now you thrive when you are helping others, expressing yourself creatively, or spending time with your family.)

Get in touch with activities you have enjoyed in the past. Magazine publisher Malcolm Forbes says, "The only [career] advice that is of any value is to do what turns you on." Many lawyers have delayed gratification for so long they're out of touch with what activities in life they really enjoy. The only way to find that joy again is to go in search of it. Remove the "shoulds" and "musts" in your life and replace them with "wants" and "likes." Start a list of happy memories from your past (see Exercise 5 in Appendix 2). Take time every evening to record the activities and experiences you most relished that day, and those you found least enjoyable.

This analysis may lead to undiscovered opportunities within the law you would find more satisfying. A career counselor for lawyers remembers one client who had a long history of being an active authority on issues of law reform. The trouble was, she had become an implementer of laws that had already been passed. It wasn't that the profession itself was inappropriate; she was simply laboring in the wrong arena. Once she voiced her need to be an activist, she was able to find another law-related job that satisfied her.

Realistically evaluate your skills. "Legal training is broad training," says New York City career counselor Celia Paul. "Fortunately, it emphasizes two skills which are invaluable to job changers: knowing how to get up to speed quickly in new areas, and the ability to sell oneself effectively in an interview." But those are not the only skills that are transferable in the marketplace.

For example, in law school casebook reading, you learn how to read and digest large quantities of obtuse, highly technical material (and many of you briefed those cases by applying skills involved with critical thinking and linear analysis). At some point during the first year, you probably wrote a Memorandum of Points and Authorities which demanded research, persuasive writing, and editing skills. By the third year, you participated in a moot court presentation which called upon skills of speaking cogently, articulately and persuasively; listening intently and critically; and thinking quickly on your feet. Equally valuable skills were developed in the classroom: dealing effectively with difficult people, and holding up under fire. Overall, after three years in the law school environment, you ended up with well-developed powers of concentration and discipline and a well-honed ability to withstand, even flourish, in a competitive environment.

In actual practice of law, lawyers display a wide variety of marketable skills. Consider:

DATA-RELATED SKILLS

Learning New Things:
    Assimilates new data quickly
    Possesses a retentive memory for rules and procedures
    Reads quickly and comprehensively
Analysis:
    Extracts and evaluates information from voluminous amounts of
       material
    Recognizes when more information is needed to make decisions
    Anticipates problems or needs before they become unmanageable
Data Handling:
    Gathers information by talking to others
    Interviews individuals to obtain information
    Recognizes the need for, and locates, outside experts

Has an accurate memory for details
Keeps track of details
Discovers similarities or dissimilarities
Classifies expertly
Files in a way to facilitate retrieval
Handles many tasks and responsibilities efficiently
Coordinates operations and details
Establishes priorities among competing requirements

Using Numbers and Financial Data:
Budgets
Maintains fiscal controls
Projects costs
Allocates scarce financial resources

Problem Solving:
Applies what others have developed to new situations
Strategizes
Makes practical applications of theoretical ideas
Plans on the basis of lessons from the past
Conceives new interpretations, concepts and approaches
Troubleshoots

Writing Technically:
Edits
Summarizes
Consolidates
Updates

Specialized Knowledge:
Familiar with medical records and terminology
Knows the intricacies of the commercial construction industry
Handles real estate purchase and sale documentation
Expert in estate and tax planning
Thoroughly acquainted with laws concerning the developmentally
  disabled

PEOPLE-RELATED SKILLS

Interpersonal Communication:
Gives out information accurately
Gains cooperation among diverse interests

Explains complicated theories or procedures in simple terms
Handles emotional outbursts
Confronts others with touchy or difficult personal matters
Trains
Employs "active listening"

Observation:
Hones and uses powers of observation
Easily remembers faces
Perceives and assesses the potential of others

Making Presentations:
Speaks clearly, articulately and engagingly
Improvises
Quickly sizes up situations
Acts on new information immediately
Deals well with the unexpected or critical event
Decisive in emergencies

Helping Others:
. Develops rapport and trust
Allays fears
Counsels
Keeps confidences and secrets
Helps to identify problems, needs and solutions
Clarifies values and goals of others
Gives professional advice
Experiments with new approaches

Persuading Others:
Sells a program or course of action to decision-makers
Negotiates

Leadership:
Brings projects in on time and within budget
Delegates authority
Supervises
Makes hard decisions

Self-Direction and Responsibility:
Follows through
Organizes one's time expertly
Continually searches for more responsibility

150

Systematically accomplishes tasks in order to obtain or surpass
   objectives
Works well without supervision

Stop delaying gratification. It began in law school. You plowed
through tomes of boring material, knowing that three years later the pay
off would be a coveted law degree. Then came the summer of suffering
to sit for the bar examination in order to get your license. Next, the
endless hours of researching arcane points of law in dusty, stuffy
environments so that you could appear in court some day or actually
meet with a client. Now that you have become a partner, and are earning
a respectable income, you put off enjoying the fruits of your labor until
"this case" settles, or "that deal" is closed. Or maybe you're already
waiting until retirement for real pleasure. Consider this: an issue of the
Washington State Bar News announced the deaths of four practicing
attorneys, two men and two women. The oldest was 42. Now, ask
yourself this question: what are you *waiting* for?

Don't put off decisions until you lose your job or get burned out. Try
to avoid the pattern seen all too often by career counselors: first, the
shock of getting fired or laid off (probably after months of denying any
job insecurity), then a few leisurely weeks off until money begins to run
out, and finally, an indiscriminate job search consisting of calls to friends
and potential employers, responses to classified ads and contacting
placement agencies, ready to take anything that is offered. Only after all
that, do you consider a proper career planning process. Unfortunately,
by then, you're probably out of time ... and money!

Or, the worst-case scenario: you succumb to burnout, evidenced by
exhaustion, cynicism, hopelessness, helplessness, and out-of-control
behavior such as drug use, drinking, workaholism, and overeating.
Lesah Beckhusen, who offers regular courses and group counseling to
lawyers in the San Francisco Bay area, says lawyers need to be alert to
the four progressive stages of burnout: mild dissatisfaction, increasing
fatigue, the first thoughts of quitting, and finally, resigning your job
without any plans. And don't regard burnout as a "failure of character."
Instead, take radical action. Beckhusen suggests a three-month sabbatical to restore health and vitality, and to get out from under the cynicism.
If that is not possible, she suggests taking a two-week vacation at home

"to build back control into your life." At a minimum, invest in an intensive course of career counseling, get lots of exercise and relaxation, and create a plan and a timeline for changes.

The moral is, start the career planning process at the first signs of trouble.

Let go of the notion that you owe a lifetime commitment to your current employer or partners, or even to your legal career. One veteran practitioner (and now a trial court judge) counsels high school students not to think about careers as 35-year commitments. Instead, she advises them to ask, "What do I want to do for the next 10 years?" Says Judge Faith Enyeart of King County Superior Court in Seattle, Washington, "We need to reorient our thinking about our careers so that we go with the flow of whatever seems to be right at the time, use it as a building experience, and then move on."

Her advice reflects a national reality: the legal profession is beginning to experience the same degree of employment mobility as the rest of white-collar America. After a century of practice as a gentleman's profession, law firms now operate like big business. Attorneys are hired, fired and traded like professional athletes. Associates not only receive no guarantees of partnership, but many are laid off shortly after they're hired because of unstable firm finances. Law partnerships are dissolving and reforming as personalities clash, goals change, or loyalties shift. In that environment, it is much less realistic for any lawyer to feel obligated to set a long-term course in the profession.

THE PLANNING PROCESS

- Invest substantial time and energy in planning.
- Don't intellectualize where to go next and how to get there.
- Ask for support.
- Be patient and persistent.
- Expect an emotional rollercoaster.
- Look for what you want, not what you think you can get.
- Thoroughly investigate the next career before taking the plunge.
- Don't seek another degree unless it is a requirement.
- Don't expect employers to clamor for your services.

- Consider rewriting your resume.
- Make a conscious choice to "pay dues" again in a new field.
- Accept the possibility of failure.

Invest substantial time and energy into planning. As Hindi Greenberg stated in Chapter 5, "A lot of people expect to hop from one job or career to another with a snap of their fingers. It doesn't work that way. It is a long, arduous process." With this in mind, start your planning process now. Enroll in career evaluation courses. Hire a career counselor. Work through the exercises in Appendix 2. Consider investing in the some of the books recommended in Appendix 4. Devote a part of every day to identifying your skills, interests and values, and how they translate into work you would enjoy.

Don't intellectualize where to go next and how to get there. Ava Butler, a Seattle-based human resources consultant with experience in career counseling for lawyers, says, "Lawyers usually want to know for sure that career planning is going to work; they want facts and evidence. That's their training. But there are so many unknowns in any career change, and it's that fear of the unknown that keeps many lawyers unhappy and stuck."

Lesah Beckhusen, another West Coast career counselor, says, "If I had to come up with the major issue that makes my job with attorneys a real challenge, it is their almost exclusively left-brained thinking about how the world works." Lawyers, she says, are trained to rely upon their left brains, the center of rational, linear, organized thought. But, human beings are motivated by what they want, not by what is logical or practical. Beckhusen suggests that lawyers ought to work on using more of their intuition and feelings to create a vision of what they want. Then, they can let their left-brain skills create a plan for getting there.

Ask for support. Dissatisfied lawyers typically receive little sympathy from family and non-lawyer friends. "The community understands social workers, nurses or teachers who want to leave their jobs," says Ava Butler. "Their work is hard and they receive so little pay. But, the general public doesn't feel much sympathy for lawyers who are perceived as being well-compensated and intellectually stimulated. Most people are incredulous, and wonder, 'What do you mean you don't want to be a lawyer?'"

This is especially true for those lawyers who come from families that identify strongly with the lawyer image. Butler has worked with attorneys who, when they tell their families that they are quitting law, end up with the mother crying, the father screaming, and siblings looking at them with a "what-the-hell-is-wrong-with-you?" attitude. Says Butler, "To get through this period, you need to have a lot of self-esteem, self-confidence and self-will."

Consider also the advice of Dr. Robert Rosen, a psychologist and president of Healthy Companies, a Virginia consulting concern that helps companies cope with discontented workers. He suggests that you seek others who have made a successful job change, and use their examples to find solutions to your own problems.[1] At the same time, find support from others who are undergoing a similar experience. Join or start a Lawyers in Transition program (see the Epilogue), or get together a discussion group with some of your friends (see Appendix 2). Find the allies you need to complete your transition.

Be patient and persistent. Perseverance and an unwavering commitment are the keys to completing a successful job transition. According to Ava Butler, this is where most lawyers fail. When work seems intolerable or especially insecure, they make a few half-hearted employment inquiries or send out a batch of resumes. When those efforts don't succeed in securing alternative employment, and their job pressures ease, they put career plans back on the shelf. A few months later, work grows unbearable again and the cycle begins anew. All career counselors agree that the job search must continue through the good times, and that it requires stamina and commitment equal to a part-time job.

Career transition also does not occur in a straight line, and it can take many years. According to Butler, "Most people feel that they are rounding one big circle over and over again as they pass through periods of excitement and depression. As a result, they stop the process after finishing a circle or two. What they are actually doing, though, is traveling in *spiraling* circles, each time getting a little closer to satisfying reemployment. If they persist, and accept a certain amount of confusion as part of the process, they find the answers they want over time."

Expect an emotional rollercoaster. You are likely to experience a wide range of emotions as you reach the decision to leave the legal profession. Ava Butler describes the process: "Denial is the first stage. Clients feel discontent, but don't know where it comes from. They say things like, 'This isn't so bad,' or 'It will get better,' or 'There's nothing I can do about it,' or 'It'll change if I can only hold out until I'm a partner,' or 'It'll be fine as soon as this case is over.' The next stage is anger — anger at themselves, the system, their colleagues, their spouses, the world, life, society, everybody. Next comes bargaining. They say, 'If I move to this or that,' or 'If I was in a different city or a different law firm or dealing with a different aspect of law,' or 'Maybe if we had a baby.' In career counseling, we often find that acceptance comes when the client decides what he or she is going to do next. Then, sadness or depression commonly follows." The point is, these emotional swings are normal. Instead of fighting them, accept them as signals of your progress.

Look for what you want, not what you think you can get. Larry Richard practiced law in Philadelphia and Manhattan for 10 years before becoming a career counselor for lawyers. His clients commonly ask, "What else is out there that I can do?" They're asking the wrong question, he says. "What they ought to be asking is, 'Who am I? What do I really want to do? What type of work, work environment, people, and activities will give me a sense of fulfillment?' The *biggest* mistake a lawyer can make is to hope to fall into something interesting without first having made a thorough evaluation and analysis of what that something ought to be."

Richard suggests you present yourself as a specialist to potential employers. "People who offer themselves as a kind of jack-of-all-trades are generally unsuccessful in their job hunt," he says. "Employers are interested in somebody who has enthusiasm and motivation, and who has formulated a game plan. They believe that a goal-directed person will apply that single-mindedness to their businesses."

Thoroughly investigate the next career before taking the plunge. Attend professional meetings. Talk to those who do what you want to do. Ask questions — the ones you probably never asked before entering law school. Acquire first-hand knowledge by attending professional meetings, subscribing to specialty magazines or newsletters, volunteering, and taking adult education courses. Learn everything you can about the new field before accepting employment in it. The benefits extend beyond the obvious. If you learn about the field by participating in it, you will also create a new network of friends who may lead you to a job in that field.

Don't seek another degree unless it is a requirement. Evaluate whether, by pursuing further formal education, you are again falling into the trap of postponing important career decisions. Investigate your target industry to determine whether a specialized advanced degree is an absolute prerequisite. It could be that apprenticing in the field for a year will get you as far as the two to three years you would otherwise spend in school.

Don't expect employers to clamor for your services. Job counselor Celia Paul finds that, "Lawyers end up buying into society's view of the profession; that they merit prestige, respect, big money, and that anything less is beneath them. I call it an 'entitlement mentality.' It's something I really have to work with. You just can't tell people that you are a lawyer and expect that to open doors (in some cases, in fact, it closes them). I teach clients that they will be hired because of their skills — not because they're lawyers — and that it's up to them to translate their skills into something marketable."

Ava Butler agrees. "Lawyers do like to feel special," she says, "and that their career issues are different. They feel that because they have paid their dues in law, that they're paid up forever. But it just isn't true. Lawyers have to go through the same hoops as everybody else; making contacts and building an image. Unfortunately, lawyers aren't comfortable marketing themselves, probably because marketing has traditionally been prohibited by professional ethics. Eventually, though, they have to learn. Like every other job hunter, they have to join new professional organizations and get known in different circles."

J. Fredric Way, associate dean at the Columbia business school, advises lawyers to be very clear about their reasons for leaving the law — both in their own minds and in explaining them to potential employers. Then, he says, they should play up experience that is applicable to a targeted job, play down what is not . . . and not play *lawyer* at all.[2]

Consider rewriting your resume. There are three basic types of resumes: *chronological, functional,* and *targeted.* Most resumes found in the legal profession are of the *chronological* variety, a listing by date of job experience, education and other relevant background. A *chronological* resume works best when you are looking for another job in the same field.

A *functional* resume organizes your relevant work, volunteer and educational history into categories, and is well-suited for someone, such as a lawyer/accountant or lawyer/writer, who wants to combine those backgrounds into one job. A *targeted* resume presents your background with another twist. It focuses on overall skills and achievements, and downplays actual experience in the industry you have targeted. For example, you might first describe your specific talents, such as effective public speaker or group facilitator, and then support your claim by listing achievements, education, and work experience relevant to your claimed expertise.

A resume should be short (preferably one page), clearly written, professionally proofread and formatted, and should include only that information which is relevant to the job for which you are applying. Personal information, inactive memberships in community or professional organizations, and recommendations (unless they are from well-known, influential people) should be omitted. Ava Butler also strongly suggests that you write your own resume. "There are services that, for a considerable fee, will do all the work," says Butler. "But they don't serve you all that well. The resume ends up representing someone else's style, and highlights only what the resume writer thinks is important about you." Another reason you ought to do it yourself, adds Butler, is that the actual process of writing a resume is a critical part of preparing for an interview.

Make a conscious choice to "pay dues" again in a new field. An attitude of humility will go a long way toward easing the trauma of moving from a prestigious job to starting fresh in a new field. It might help to join the available professional organizations and participate in their committees to create a network of new business acquaintances. Or, volunteer or apprentice on a part-time basis. The "dues paying" stage can be an extended process, requiring you to remain in your current job or to take a temporary position, while working toward what you really want. One former practitioner secured a non-legal position as director of a mediation program after spending close to three years volunteering as an arbitrator.

Accept the possibility of failure. The fear of the unknown keeps many unhappy lawyers stuck in their dissatisfaction. You may worry that if you start to evaluate your likes and dislikes, you will discover that nothing in law will ever be satisfying or that you'll have to move to a different city or give up your current lifestyle. Worse yet, you might have to face the fact that you may not achieve the success you crave in the field you choose. All of these fears are completely normal. A note of encouragement, however: you are more likely to succeed in any field about which you feel passionately. But you'll never know for certain until you accept the risk of finding out.

POSTSCRIPT TO THE PROFESSION

- Don't close doors behind you.
- Continue to invest in your own fulfillment.

Don't close doors behind you. There's no point bad-mouthing those still operating within the profession, or even the profession itself. You may want to return some day. And, says ex-practitioner Arnold Patent, "Until you are clear that you will never again use your license, maintain it." (Note: With only one exception, the non-practicing attorneys interviewed for this book have all maintained a license to practice in at least one state.)

Continue to invest in your own fulfillment. In a Buddhist fable, a man trips off a ledge but grabs a sturdy branch before falling to his death. As he clings to the branch, the man frantically looks around and sees a grassy plateau that might cushion his fall. But it appears to be way beyond his reach. Suddenly, a voice booms, "Let go of the branch and jump. You can make it!"

The man is perplexed. He wants to trust the voice and jump, but he's afraid he'll miss his target and die. On the other hand, dangling from a branch for the rest of his life makes no sense either. Over and over again, he debates his options, all the while hanging in limbo.

What does it finally take for him to accept the instructions of the voice?

A simple leap of faith.

Kevin Ward, author of *Not the Official Lawyers Handbook*, CEO of a New York corporate communications company, and himself a former practicing attorney, puts it very simply:

"Jump," he says. "You can fly."

Appendix Two:
Getting Together With Other Lawyers in Transition

E very lawyer has those qualities necessary to effect a career change: persistence, a sense of responsibility and a history of success in achieving goals. But sometimes, the mere thought of getting through the process can be daunting. Often, it seems easier to let current professional demands take priority, or just to give up when sending out a few resumes and making a few telephone calls do not yield measurable results. But there's only one way to develop more satisfying work. You must stick to it.

FINDING SUPPORT

To help with what promises to be a very taxing process, first begin by reaching out to people who accept your decision to leave the profession. Some of you already have that kind of support in place. Others, though, may be surrounded by friends, relatives and colleagues who find it difficult to accept that being a lawyer is no longer satisfying to you. No matter how important these people are in the rest of your life, they should not be depended upon to assist you in your career change process. Instead, look for others who are willing to discard — or, better yet, have no — preexisting notions about you; who are strong enough to challenge you when you head in the wrong direction, and who are also compassionate enough simply to be there when things get rough.

It wouldn't hurt to look for people who are also well-connected and who would be willing to share their contacts to help you on your way.

At this stage, your best bet is to seek out a network of support from other disaffected attorneys. The most direct way to create this network is to contact all those practitioners who have mentioned to you their dissatisfaction. These individuals may not be interested in exploring the issue now, but they might know someone else who is. Keep at it until you have found at least three other practitioners who are interested in meeting regularly for career evaluation and support.

If you don't know anybody who is unhappy with law, or if you are afraid to bring up the subject, place a notice in your local bar association publication. For example:

> *Practicing attorney seeks to meet weekly with other practitioners for career evaluation, discussion and support. All inquiries held in strictest confidence.*

List your home telephone number and perhaps your first name, and the best time of day to reach you. Some callers will be skittish about leaving a message on an unknown answering machine, so make certain that you are available to answer the telephone personally.

Select a mutually agreeable meeting day and decide both the starting and finishing times of each get-together. Experience has shown that frequent meetings keep everyone's momentum going. One-and-a-half to two hours per week is ideal. Early evening hours work well for most lawyers; but breakfast or lunch meetings might be equally convenient. Just be certain that the participants' law practices will not regularly interfere with the chosen day and hour.

As for your meeting place, a word of caution: it would probably be inappropriate to meet in the conference room of your law office, or on bar association property, because of the sensitivity of the discussion. Many libraries, community centers, law schools and high schools offer free use of their facilities to community groups. Of course, if a private home, or a discreetly-located office, is available, so much the better.

At the first meeting, take the time to get acquainted with the other members of the group. Share your backgrounds and complaints about work. Discuss what each person hopes to get out of the meetings. But don't spend more than one meeting on the "why" questions: that is, why am I resistant to making a change? Why did I go into law school in the first place? Why do I dislike my work so much? Why didn't I leave five years ago?

Concentrate instead on the who, what, where, when, and how questions. For example:

Who can I count on for support in making a career change? *Who* can I talk to about some of my job ideas?

What is important to me? *What* would I rather be doing than practicing law?

Where am I willing to live and/or work? *Where* can I find resources to give me more information about industries that interest me?

When am I going to quit my job? *When* does the professional organization in the field I've targeted hold its meetings?

How can I turn my legal background into a fulfilling job in another industry? *How* should I break the news to my family? *How* can I reshuffle my obligations so that I have more time and energy to pursue a career change?

Avoid turning your meetings into gripe sessions, though. Instead, agree on a format which encourages positive forward movement. Offer telephone check-in's as the need arises. For this purpose, and also to notify the other members if you will be unable to attend a meeting, circulate a list of names and message phone numbers for everyone in the group.

Support will mean something different to each person in the group and will vary at different stages in their transitions. Sometimes, it will mean urging others on, offering a sincere "You can do it," or "Don't give up." Other times, the situation may call for bluntness about the seeming inappropriateness of the path a group member has taken. To assure that you get meaningful help, be honest with yourself about the kind of feedback that works for you and ask for that type of input when you feel stuck. The success of the group may well depend on how well you and the others learn to give and receive support.

SUGGESTED CAREER ASSESSMENT FORMAT

Every successful job or career change begins with a period of honest soul-searching. To complete this part of the process, you must isolate and define those things you enjoy and dislike both in your current employment and your life in general. In this way, you can locate work that makes use of the skills, values, aptitudes, and interests you find satisfying. Without this kind of careful analysis, career change is nothing more than a toss of the dice. Career counselors refer to this process of self-examination as the "self-assessment" or "clarification" stage of career planning.

The following format, to be completed with a group of three to seven other attorneys, begins the process of defining career direction. These exercises are designed to reveal what you find enjoyable and objectionable in five areas: values, interests, skills, and physical and people environments. The format depends upon group feedback, and calls upon skills commonly held by lawyers such as listening critically, drawing conclusions, evaluating information, and clarifying values and goals for others.

Every week, the members of the group orally present their "homework" assignment. Then, as each person speaks, the others carefully record the statements, implications, and observations they believe bear on the speaker's preferences, values, interests, competencies, and motivations.

GUIDELINES FOR PARTICIPATION IN THE WORKSHOP

Rely upon your intuition. Share your immediate and spontaneous reactions and opinions. Do not censor your conclusions or impressions because you haven't any tangible proof. Express whatever comes to your mind. If you can, incorporate your recollections from prior weeks with what you are hearing that day. Remember that your observations are not "right" or "wrong." They are simply "feedback" to be considered and ultimately accepted, rejected, or modified by the speaker alone.

Avoid being judgmental. This is perhaps the most difficult task for a group of lawyers trained to decide what's "right and wrong," and "good and bad." The best listeners simply monitor what is being said, and then synthesize, restate or draw conclusions about the themes they hear. But refrain from adding value judgments to your observations. For example, such comments as "You don't have to fight when you're a litigator," or "I think you have unrealistic expectations about practicing law," are not appropriate.

Avoid providing solutions. This admonishment applies not only to your interaction with other group members, but to your own participation in the workshop. Refrain (until the brainstorming session later) from remarks such as, "You should get out of trial work," or "I know the perfect job for you."

Accept emotional outbursts as part of the process. Occasionally, a speaker will express strong emotions. Someone may cry or be unable to finish a presentation in an effort to maintain control. Let the speaker be. Do not give advice, or attempt to fix the situation, or offer analysis, or tell him what he should have done or should be feeling. The point of the exercises is to begin discovering what those emotions might mean in terms of job preferences, not to repair the speaker's relationship with his or her work.

Complete the program before you take the next step. Avoid drawing conclusions about your career direction until you have gathered all the information this process will provide. If you can, postpone any decision to resign from your job or accept another one (unless, of course, finances demand it).

TELL THE TRUTH, both to yourself and to the other group members. The awareness you develop by participating in this process will only be as helpful as the accuracy of the information you provide.

EXERCISE #1

HOMEWORK: Come to the next meeting prepared to tell the group about one good experience (joyful, engaging, satisfying, fulfilling) and one bad experience (uncomfortable, trying, aggravating, depressing, frustrating) in your legal career. You know you're on the right track by the strength of your emotional reaction. One ought to lift your spirits;

the other may trigger anger, sorrow or shame.

In making your selections, consider only the process, and not the end result. For example, if you remember a particular trial as a peak experience because you won against all odds — but the experience of trying the case was unpleasant and full of negative stresses — don't pick that trial as a "good experience." Instead, think about it as a bad one. Likewise, if you ended up with a terrible result on a case, but you thoroughly enjoyed the client and the legal issues, consider that a "good experience."

Also, try not to pick events that stand out in your memory mostly because of the outside response you received. Everyone feels badly when criticized and good when praised. So when you choose events which depend upon the criticism or kudos of others, you don't learn very much about your unique character and preferences.

Don't spend too much time trying to figure out the very best examples in both categories; you might even want to pick the first examples that come to your mind. But do be specific. NOTE: Do not select general areas of practice or types of skills such as, "I can't think of one good experience but I know I like being in trial."

AT THE MEETING: Each person, in turn, describes the details of the two experiences. Relate the chronology, starting with the most immediate events of that day or week. Devote only a couple sentences to background information such as the legal issues involved or your prior encounters with this same type of problem or person. But be as descriptive as you can about specific conversations, the nature of the work, conflicts and encounters, while avoiding your own conclusions about what made the experiences good or bad. The rest of the group must listen carefully, and record the themes they hear.

The group makes certain that each speaker's selection satisfies the homework instructions. That is, the focus should be on the process and not the result, and two *specific* experiences should be shared. If the speaker should draw a blank, ask that person to pick two experiences that occurred that day or week; one which was relatively positive and the other relatively negative.

If questions are necessary at the end of a presentation, ask them for clarification purposes only. Do not cross-examine the speaker, nor attempt to get him or her to confirm your intuitions. For example, you might suspect that, in general, the speaker doesn't like to argue with others. Instead of asking the speaker whether your hunch is accurate, or asking him how he would describe a bad relationship, simply write down your conclusion. On the other hand, if the speaker never mentioned anything about other people, you may ask him or her who, if anyone else, was involved in the experience.

Allow each person at least 10 minutes. If time permits, questions may be posed at the end of each person's presentation. Afterwards, the speaker receives the written notes of the others. These notes will be used later in the process and should be saved.

EXERCISE #2

HOMEWORK: Read quickly through a *Time, Newsweek, U.S. News & World Report* or other general interest magazine. Select the six articles you found the most interesting and/or intriguing, and which you read from beginning to end. The articles can be of any length. A feature page dealing with a common topic, such as "People" or the "Week in Review," may be considered one article, or you may break it down into several articles. If you can't find six articles you really enjoyed, select another magazine until you come up with a full half-dozen. Bring all six articles, or photocopies, to the next meeting.

AT THE MEETING: This exercise, as well as the next three, follow the same general format as the first, except that the speaker receives both written and oral feedback.

In this exercise, each member is asked to point out what was interesting, appealing, intriguing, or thought-provoking, about the articles he or she selected. The other members of the group must listen carefully and record key words and phrases to reflect the themes, preferences, patterns, values, and interests they either intuit or hear directly. Remember, record your hunches and intuitions as well as the obvious statements.

When the speaker has finished, ask open-ended questions to clarify. Then, the group discusses their observations, pointing out the themes and patterns they find in each individual article and in all of them when taken as a whole. As the members share their observations, the speaker writes down *everything* that is said and does not participate in the discussion. That means not attempting to clarify what you said so that the listeners get it "right."

Spend 15 minutes per person, divided about equally for explanation of the articles, questions, and oral feedback. Before moving on to the next presentation, hand your written comments to the speaker.

EXERCISE #3

HOMEWORK: This time, find a pictorial magazine such as *LIFE*, *Sunset*, or *Vogue* (one you don't mind tearing apart). The magazine may concentrate on one subject or special interest, but it must include both color and black-and-white photographs (editorial or advertising) and be relatively new.

Skim through the magazine, marking each picture that makes you pause or stop as you turn the pages. Next, go back through the pictures you have marked and quickly select the six you find most visually striking, provocative or appealing. Tear out these six pictures and bring them to the next meeting. NOTE: Do not select a picture because it became more intriguing after you read the caption. Instead, select pictures that appeal to you visually, without any explanation.

AT THE MEETING: Each person describes the pictures he or she selected, pointing out what was most appealing, engaging, intriguing, disturbing, or pleasing about them in terms of color, layout, perspective, subject matter, mood, and other visual elements. Once again, the group is asked to listen carefully, noting their observations on paper. After the speaker has explained each picture, spread the collection out so everyone can see all of the pictures well. Then, the group discusses what they see are the patterns, interests, preferences and values in each individual picture as well as in the selection as a whole, taking into consideration the speaker's expressed perspective. NOTE: Sometimes a speaker will find a picture comforting or calming that others in the group find disturbing. Or, the speaker will notice details that most of the others didn't see. Observations such as these can lead to interesting discussions about the speaker's preferences.

The speaker records all of the group's insights and observations. Allow at least 15 minutes per person. As before, the group's written observations are given to the speaker.

EXERCISE #4

HOMEWORK: Review the "Help Wanted" section of the Sunday newspaper. As you read through the first time, circle every advertisement that appeals to you for any reason, without consideration of either salary or qualifications. Now, take a closer look at all the ads you've circled, and clip out between a half-dozen and a dozen that continue to have appeal. Next, write an ad for your fantasy job, describing in detail the work you would love to do. Let your imagination go and assume the job would pay a salary which supports you and your family in a comfortable lifestyle. You may consider tangibles such as location, work hours, and vacation allotment if they are crucial to you. But, don't include salary or qualifications. Bring the newspaper advertisements, as well as your fantasy ad, to the next meeting.

AT THE MEETING: Each person shares his or her collection of classified ads with the group, and explains what elements were so appealing. (Sharing the fantasy ad with the group is optional.) Follow the same format as the prior weeks, writing down observations as the speaker is talking and then discussing those observations while the speaker records all of the feedback.

EXERCISE #5

HOMEWORK: Jot down 50 of the most enjoyable experiences of your life. They should be ones you remember as absorbing, fun, rewarding and/or fulfilling; events during which time passed by without notice because you were so thoroughly engaged. Choose events you enjoyed as they were unfolding, not because of the good result you attained, or because you received positive feedback or reinforcement. An event may be something as simple as a memorable sunset, or as unforgettable as a vacation to Greece. When choosing a more complex event, isolate the high points and consider each one a separate experience. Include at least 10 experiences from your childhood — fingerpainting, playing games, your first camping trip, whatever! The point is to get back in touch with experiences that lifted your spirits, were easy and fun, and which you would gladly repeat.

Then write a list of 10 awful experiences — when time dragged or was filled with frustration, dread and/or fear; experiences you would never choose to repeat. Again, consider only the process and not the result.

When both lists are complete, spend at least an hour answering the following questions as they apply to each set of experiences:

1. How often were you alone and how often with others? What were you doing when you were alone? How did those activities differ from the times when you were with others?

2. How many others were with you? What was the nature of your interaction with them? Were you conversing or participating with them, or quietly working alongside them? Were you engaged in some group activity? What kind?

3. What were the personality characteristics of the other people around you? Up-beat? Analytical? Responsible? Daring? Supportive? Competitive? Challenging? Smart? Artistic? Athletic?

4. What were you doing? Was it physical, mental, both? Were you passive or active, moving or staying in one place? Conveying or receiving information?

5. What was the purpose of your participation in each event? Personal growth, building something, enjoyment for the sake of enjoyment, competition?

6. In what environments did you find yourself? Indoors or outside, sunny, rainy, dark, bright, crowded, spacious, formal, informal?

7. Were you relating emotionally, intellectually, physically and/or spiritually to your surroundings?

8. Were your activities internalized, that is, thoughtful or meditative, or external to yourself — teaching, advising, coaching, viewing entertainment?

9. What was the tempo of each event? Fast-paced, relaxed, both?

Note that the answers to these questions may be contradictory. You may enjoy both being alone and being with others, or engaging in high energy activities and sitting peacefully outside in the sunshine.

AT THE MEETING: Share with the group those experiences that stand out in your memory. Talk about as many of them as you want in five or six minutes. You may pick all good experiences, all bad, or some of each. As in meetings past, the group will record its impressions, and then provide oral feedback while the speaker takes notes. Once again, accept the analysis without judgment or comment.

THE IDEAL JOB GRID

Now comes the process of consolidating all the feedback into a statement of your ideal job. Remember, this grid represents the extremes — the very best and very worst qualities — of the best job you could possibly have. The process takes several hours to complete.

The first step is to review the sample ideal job grids included here to get an idea of the kind of end-product you want to create. Then, review the feedback you accumulated from the preceding five exercises, and pull out words and phrases that have been repeated more than once, or ones which otherwise attract you. Next, place those words and phrases into the most appropriate category: interests, skills, values, people and environment.

Interests are subject matters. Skills are things you do. Values are those qualities which make the work meaningful to you. People refers to the numbers and character traits of the people you encounter as well as the amount of regular contact you want to have with others. Environment includes physical characteristics such as the location and set up of the office, and also somewhat more intangible qualities such as work style and office organization.

The first time through, you will probably have dozens of entries under some categories, and none in others. The same descriptive term may be repeated in several places. The next step is to weed out repetition by including a term only in the most appropriate category. Also, do not put opposites of the same type of quality both in the "Must Have" and "Must Avoid" columns. For example, under "Environment," either state that you want a light and spacious atmosphere on the "Must Have" side or put on the "Must Avoid" side that you don't want an overly congested workplace. But do not include both.

After you have deleted repetitive entries, evaluate the remaining words and phrases. Delete any to which you respond neutrally, with one exception: be certain to include any themes that emerged throughout all five exercises. Also, do not exclude an interest or skill because you either cannot imagine how you'd get paid to do it, or because you are

SAMPLE IDEAL JOB GRID #1

	MUST HAVE	**MUST AVOID**
INTERESTS (subject matters)	adult education human behavior houses	

SKILLS (things you do)	influencing others
	teaching/speaking
	creativity/start-up
	leading
	writing
	learning new things
		maintaining or managing
		  an established program
		purely intellectual
		  pursuits

VALUES (what makes the work meaningful)	continuing personal
	  growth
	variety
	tangible products
	challenge
	autonomy
		adversarial relationships
		doing it only for the
		  money
		 being required to
		  follow others' notions
		  of right and wrong

PEOPLE	open-minded adults
	humorous
	working independently,
	  but with others around
	feeling connected with
	  other people
		negative
		limiting
		hostile

ENVIRONMENT	light, open, spacious
	access to outdoors
	flexible hours
	complex but
	  harmonious
		smoky air
		compulsiveness/
		  workaholism
		inflexible, continuous
		  deadlines

SAMPLE IDEAL JOB GRID #2

	MUST HAVE	**MUST AVOID**
INTERESTS (subject matters)	nature/the outdoors literature financial planning & investing	
SKILLS (things you do)	communication/ writing information gathering organizing analyzing problem solving	menial clerical tasks such as typing, answering phones extemporaneous speaking
VALUES (what makes the work meaningful)	intellectual stimulation learning new things finished products	
PEOPLE	congenial cooperative working independently trustworthy & honest	adversarial/contentious
ENVIRONMENT	uncrowded comfortable private reasonable hours	unpredictable deadlines smoke-filled interminable projects

afraid it means you have to change jobs, go back to school, or take a pay cut. Make certain that anything you include is a "must;" an element that if absent would make your job less enjoyable or, if consistently there, would make it intolerable.

Also refrain from including work by-products such as "enjoying my work," "feeling like I'm contributing to society," "fulfillment," or "work that is meaningful to me." And avoid ambiguous terms that might have a different meaning for you than for the other members of the group. For example, "professionalism" could as easily imply that you simply wish to wear a suit and tie and carry a briefcase, as work in a highly ethical environment. Instead, make use of the skills in semantics you developed in law school to choose the word or phrase which precisely conveys your requirements. (A thesaurus might be helpful here.)

Notice that the grid does not include the level of compensation you require for your next position. Just assume you would earn as much money as you need to support yourself and your family.

Before the next meeting, create a grid that represents fairly accurately what you prefer in a work environment by including up to six entries per category. If no strong preference stands out for a category, leave that slot blank. Then bring to the next meeting enough copies of your grid for everyone in the group.

AT THE MEETING: The goal of this meeting is to clean up and clarify everyone's ideal job grid. To achieve that end, each person, in turn, reads quickly through the rough draft of his or her grid, explaining further any entries that are not clear to the group. Then, the group works with each person to find substitute words and phrases for those qualifications that aren't stated clearly, and to delete any remaining repetition.

When everyone is satisfied that the grid is understandable and non-repetitive, the group asks each speaker two questions: are there any "must haves" or "must avoids" that are missing from this overview? Have any been included that, upon reconsideration, are not essential and can be deleted? Both questions are designed to assure that everything in the grid is a "must," and that no crucial interests, skills, values or environmental factors have been deleted. By the end of the meeting, each member of the group should have received concrete suggestions about how the grid could be simpler, more straightforward, and more easily interpreted while still being an accurate representation of an ideal job.

OPTION BUILDING THROUGH GROUP BRAINSTORMING

Before the next meeting, you should revise, if necessary, and rewrite your ideal job grid. Then, bring copies for everyone to the next meeting.

AT THE MEETING: Since you have now finished the first step of career planning — self-assessment — you are ready to begin the next … option building. This process starts with group brainstorming.

The first rule of brainstorming is to *take off your lawyer hat*! Lawyers tend to look at problem solving logically, rationally, and critically. But brainstorming works best when ideas flow uncensored and without evaluation. The point is to be as creative as possible. Share even the most frivolous or off-the-wall suggestions. You never know where the thread of a good idea will begin.

Do not be concerned with monetary compensation, or educational or experiential requirements, or whether or not such a position actually exists. Suggest specific job titles and tasks as well as potential employers. Be sure to include law and law-related jobs if they make sense, but don't limit your suggestions to those positions. Circus clown, garbageman, President of the United States; anything goes! Just study each other's job grid and let your imaginations run wild.

One person is selected, or volunteers, to be the brainstorm umpire. This person makes certain that no commentary, analysis, criticism, discounting, or skepticism blocks the creative process. Statements such as "I'm not sure this really fits what you have there," or "You probably wouldn't make any money doing this," or "I don't know if you have the personality for this," or "There probably isn't much of a market for this," are out of bounds. Again, anything goes.

Each speaker listens without comment and *records every idea suggested.* In 10 to 15 minutes, you should each end up with at least 20 different job ideas.

AFTERTHOUGHTS ON IDEAL JOB GRID BRAINSTORMING

If you feel lukewarm toward most of the ideas you received, one of two conditions probably exists: either you are burned out or depressed, or your grid does not accurately represent your preferences. It might, instead, depict what you think you should enjoy, or what you think you could get, or what you suspect you could be paid to do. Those limitations do not serve you, and you need to revise your grid until it reflects your real passions. In order to do so, ask yourself the following questions:

- What do I like to do when I'm not working?
- What fascinates me?
- How would I spend my time if I didn't have to worry about money?
- What other jobs or projects in my past have fascinated and motivated me and what were their elements?
- What is important to me?
- If I could "fix" anything in the world, what would it be?

Then, reexamine your grid carefully to determine whether it is consistent with the answers to those questions. You might also ask someone else in the group to review the feedback you received and ascertain if you have overlooked anything. Then, revise your grid and ask the group to brainstorm again.

If burnout — evidenced by exhaustion, cynicism, hopelessness, helplessness, and out-of-control behavior such as drug use, drinking, workaholism, and overeating — sounds like your problem, read *Burn Out: Overcoming the High Cost of Success*, by Dr. Herbert Freudenberger. If possible, take a sabbatical, or even a two-week vacation, to give you time for introspection and help restore your sense of well-being.

If you are depressed, get help from a psychologist, psychiatrist, or other trained counselor; attend a personal effectiveness or transformational seminar, or seek out religious or spiritual instruction. An excellent book on this subject is Dr. David Burns' *Feeling Good.*

CONTINUING GROUP SUPPORT

From here on, each member of the group will be at a different stage in his or her career change. One might need help revising the ideal job grid. Another will ask for more brainstorming. Others will want to investigate the most appealing options. A few may even be ready to pursue a specific job.

Challenge each person to look critically at his or her choices. For example, if one participant appears to have targeted a stable and staid job that yields a high income, while his grid shows a clear preference for the risky and creative, help him weigh his values. What is truly more important to him: security and status or personal fulfillment? This is a time when the group members can make suggestions, based on what they now know about the speaker. For example, "I've heard you say over and over again that you love to help people, but it looks like you've picked a career in which you would be isolated from others most of the time. Have you thought about that?" Again, remember that there is no right or wrong. Friendly and supportive cross-examination will either strengthen the speaker's commitment to the choice, or restart the questioning process.

To accommodate the varying needs of the group, the meeting format should become more fluid and flexible. Continue to focus attention on each person for an equal share of the meeting, but let the needs of the individual dictate the content and approach of his or her presentation. Have every person spend a couple of minutes bringing the others up to date and describing possible next steps. If an individual seems to be encountering difficulties, brainstorming could be in order. (*Wishcraft*, by Barbara Sher, has good suggestions for running brainstorming sessions.) At the conclusion of each presentation, every member ought to make a commitment to action.

Appendix 1 provides an idea of possible next steps for those who wish to pursue or investigate some of the brainstormed ideas. But some participants will complete the self-assessment and evaluation process and still not feel that they have found the "right" target. Often, the problem is not that they haven't discovered what they would love to do next, but that they aren't in a state of mind to accept it. If the cause is burnout, or lack of self-confidence, that person needs to heal emotionally before making progress. For these people, some type of therapy — individual or group; enrolling in a transformational seminar; or regularly participating in a 12 Step Program — could be in order.

The support group ought to continue until every person has taken the career change process one step further. The next step could, of course, be entering a new career or taking another job, but it could also be participating in enjoyable volunteer work, pursuing a hobby, or enrolling in an educational program. Resolving to accept the status quo can also be a constructive step.

Career development is a life-long process, and any well-thought-out job change requires substantial time and energy. Former practitioners have commonly taken over a year to effect the first step of their change; those making major switches have waited up to a decade to see the results. The point is to let go of your self-imposed limitations, and persist. If you hold on to your vision of an ideal job, actively pursue it, and gather support around you, you'll eventually achieve your goals.

Appendix Three:
With the Benefit of Hindsight

PRE-LAW EVALUATION AND PLANNING

- Do some career planning before applying to law school.
- Analyze whether lawyering is likely to suit you.
- Research the realities of a legal career before settling on a law school education.
- Familiarize yourself with the actual law school experience.

Do some career planning before applying to law school. Are you looking at law school as a respectable way to put off making a career decision? Are you seeking a law degree as a kind of Ph.D. in general studies that will qualify you for a professional position outside the legal profession? The experiences of others prove that neither make very solid reasons to head to law school.

Before applying to any professional school, take advantage of the services provided by your college career services office; visit a professional career counselor; enroll in a career evaluation and planning course; or study one of the books recommended in Appendix 4. Spend time evaluating your likes and dislikes, aptitudes, interests and skills to determine what kind of work will be most personally satisfying and fulfilling. It's only after you get in touch with your own personal work goals that you will be able to evaluate how realistic a legal education will be.

Analyze whether lawyering is likely to suit you. Consider this personality preference quiz:

1. Do you like to get emotionally involved with your work?
2. Do you dislike or attempt to avoid conflict?
3. In resolving conflict, do you prefer deciding what's fair based on the circumstances of each situation?
4. Do you like to create or start projects and let others finish and/or maintain them?
5. Do you dislike paying attention to details?
6. Do you prefer short-term projects?
7. Do you value efficiency?
8. Do you like to do things your own way, on your own schedule, and in order of your own priorities?
9. Do you get more satisfaction being part of a team than being a solo act?
10. Do you want to change the world?

A "yes" answer to any of the above questions ought to raise serious reservations about the wisdom of entering law school, and especially about planning to use your degree to practice law. Larry Richard, owner of *LAWGISTICS*, the Philadelphia-based consulting firm, contends that practicing law is attractive to people whose main enjoyment is dealing with important issues and theories; that, in his words, "Law is the ultimate cognitive satisfier." He also believes that a legal career is almost instantly satisfying to people who like detail. According to another source, a legal career is most suitable for someone who places the highest premium on external rewards such as compensation, status and security; while there is little room in law for unrestrained creativity. Those of you who thrive on interpersonal interaction, teamwork, or helping others, may find frustrating the emphasis on research, writing and legal analysis. There may be some appropriate options for you in the legal profession, but it does call for more thorough research. Read carefully through the stories in Chapter 4, and follow these additional suggestions before plunging forward.

Research the realities of a legal career before deciding on law school. The stylized media images presented by "Perry Mason," "L.A. Law," or any of the recent Hollywood films on lawyering, do not accurately portray the real-life practice of law. In fact, very few of the day-to-day activities of law practice are as glamorous and consistently stimulating as on the screen. In the first few years, especially, much of the work can be tedious and repetitive. Ordinarily, inexperienced law firm associates devote most of their time to researching, writing, and drafting pleadings and contracts. Only a few years later do they earn the privilege of interacting with clients, appearing in court, or delegating to subordinates the myriad details that drive less meticulous practitioners mad.

Instead of depending on fiction, go directly to the source. Both *Rees*, featured in Chapter 3, and *Phil*, featured in Chapter 8, urge you to apprentice in a law firm or courthouse for two years. Talk to many lawyers; those who enjoy practicing and those who do not. Talk to criminal prosecutors and defenders, civil litigators for the plaintiff and the defendant, corporate attorneys, tax specialists, divorce lawyers. Ask these practitioners to describe their typical week. Better yet, arrange to spend an entire day with one of them.

Familiarize yourself with the actual law school experience. Make a point of sitting in on a few law school classes. Pick up a law school textbook and study it. Talk to current law students and recent graduates. Ask them what value law school is having for them now, and what realistic opportunities await them.

TIPS FOR LAW STUDENTS AND RECENT GRADUATES

- Resist pressure to enter private practice from law school.
- Find a work environment that will satisfy your needs.

Resist pressure to enter private practice from law school. Many students enter law school determined to apply their law degrees to purposes other than private practice. By the time they graduate, however, the majority (65 percent, according to the National Association for Law Placement; up to 85 percent of graduates from top law schools) have funnelled into law firms. Although the high salaries and security of these positions are attractive (and you might be able to justify a detour from your true goals by assuring yourself the experience will create options for the future), be aware that those same justifications can also become traps. Unhappy practitioners agree that it is very difficult — both emotionally and practically — to make a change that has the appearance of stepping down the ladder of success. Therefore, if you entered law to have a positive impact on either individuals or on society, find a position that satisfies that desire. In that way, you will find out right away whether lawyering will satisfy your altruistic urges. But, if you thought a legal education would broaden your *business* skills, start your career in that arena instead.

Find a work environment that will satisfy your needs. The questions on the following pages will help you target the type of legal work that most appeals to you. Before you answer the questions, however, make sure you are responding to your own feelings, and not to what you believe would most impress others or meet the expectations of your family, friends, or colleagues. Once you have answered all of the questions, and have a clearer vision of your preferences, incorporate the answers into a description of your ideal legal position. Then, begin to research the job market to locate jobs that fit that image.

1. **WHAT ARE YOUR WORK VALUES?** Pick as many as apply but rate them in order of importance to you.

___to help people   ___to earn a good living

___to help businesses   ___to "do good"

___to meet intellectual challenges   ___to develop friendships

___to study thoroughly points of law   ___to make new laws

___to create agreement   ___to win

___to solve problems   ___to be influential

___to excel   ___other:_____

2. **WHERE ARE YOU WILLING TO WORK?** Pick as many as apply but rate them in order of importance to you.

___out of my home   ___central business district

___in a rural area   ___in my neighborhood

___suburban business district   ___foreign country

___anywhere in the U. S   ___only in certain cities

3. HOW MUCH CONTROL OVER YOUR WORK ENVIRONMENT DO YOU WANT?

___owner

___mid-level manager

___supervised employee

___part of a team

___freelance

___senior manager

___unsupervised employee

___consultant

___contract worker

4. WHAT COMPENSATION ARRANGEMENT DO YOU PREFER?

___salaried

___contingent

___incentive bonus

___share of profits

___other:_____

___hourly

___retainer

___stock options

___commissions

5. WHAT SIZE GROUP IS MOST COMFORTABLE TO YOU?

___by myself

___5 to 15 people

___41 to 150 people

___space-sharing arrangement

___under 5 people

___16 to 40 people

___more than 150 people

6. WHAT TASK(S) DO YOU WANT TO ACCOMPLISH? Pick as many as apply, but rate them in order of importance to you.

___taking depositions

___lead attorney in jury trials

___assisting attorney in trials

___negotiating

___investigating

___advising people

___"rainmaking"

___motions court appearances

___lead attorney in court trials

___document coordinator

___legal research and writing

___interviewing

___advising businesses

___preparing witnesses

___advocating positions   ___drafting documents

___managing clerical staff   ___managing cases

___managing professional staff   ___managing client services

___training people   ___strategizing

___completing forms   ___lobbying

___financial analysis   ___office administration

___law library management

___other:_____

7. WHAT SUBJECT MATTER(S) APPEAL TO YOU?

___personal injury   ___business deals

___domestic relations   ___estate planning

___environmental law   ___land use planning

___administrative law   ___franchising

___taxation   ___ethics

___medical malpractice   ___products liability

___insurance   ___entertainment

___sports   ___patent

___computers   ___antitrust

___poverty law   ___utilities

___interstate transportation   ___banking

___bankruptcy   ___admiralty and maritime

___civil rights   ___women's rights

___worker's compensation   ___landlord/tenant

___creditor/debtor   ___libel and slander

___health care   ___securities regulation

___intellectual property   ___constitutional issues

___probate and guardianship   ___trademark and copyright

___criminal prosecution or defense   ___juvenile dependency

___law office economics   ___other:_____

HOW TO DEVELOP CAREER SATISFACTION AS A LAWYER

- Network to find mentors whose style you want to emulate.
- Express your own values and notions of right and wrong.
- Be conscious of the way your legal training can negatively impact your personal life.
- Preserve time for yourself, your family, your hobbies and contribution to your community.
- If your current job does not fit your personality, your skills or your interests, find one that does.
- Look at career development as a process.

Network to find mentors whose style you want to emulate. You can find mentors in any organization of lawyers. But you might begin your search in the organization in which you are employed, or in your local bar association. Another excellent option is to participate in an American Inn of Court, which describes itself as a "community-based legal organization dedicated to promoting continuing improvement of the skills, ethics and professionalism of trial and appellate advocates in an atmosphere of collegiality." For more information about the American Inn of Court nearest you, write 1225 Eye Street, N.W., Suite 300, Washington, D.C. 20005, or telephone (202) 682-1613.

Express your own values and notions of right and wrong. Resist pressure to conform to a style of lawyering unsuitable to you, or that violates your sense of fair play and diplomacy. Part of this process is learning how to say "no;" taking the risk of disappointing or angering your clients, your employer, and other attorneys. If the action you are asked to take makes you cringe, say "no." If your co-workers' ethics and attitudes offend you, and your employer requires you to adopt a similar style, find another job.

Be conscious of the way your legal training can negatively impact your personal life. "Lawyers are trained to separate their feelings from the position the client wants them to take," says one former practitioner. "That serves you well as a lawyer, but it is lousy for you as a human being." Approaches that bring success in the legal profession are often inappropriate — or even destructive — when applied to personal relationships. In an article in *Barrister* entitled "Do Lawyers Have Problems Being People," Dr. Barry A. Goodfield commented, "when victory is at the expense of clear and honest communication, when the logic and verbal skills gained and honed through training and practice are used to succeed or to overcome the opponent, when different views become the basis for defense and attack," personal relationships deteriorate. In order to maintain a balance between their personal and professional lives, Dr. Goodfield recommends that lawyers "hold off judgment until the last possible moment," get regular psychological check-ups, look at the ultimate goal in life as enjoying the process, and place as much emphasis on qualities of affection and well-being as on influence, skill, responsibility and wealth.

Preserve time for yourself, your family, your hobbies and contribution to your community. You will likely sacrifice some money in the process, since there are only so many billable hours in a day. But the inner satisfaction you receive in the long run will pay off more than meeting the challenge of 20-hour work days at the expense of your personal interests and relationships. In Washington, D.C., the Project on Adult Lives suggests that connecting spiritually with the larger world, finding ways to express your creativity, and restoring ethnic identification, family bonds, or social activism to your life, will result in the continued renewal of happiness and satisfaction.

If your current job does not fit your personality, your skills or your interests, find another. Career development is a process, and each position can be a stepping stone toward the right job for you. But don't fall into the trap of taking just any new job to escape the discomfort of the old one. Instead, carefully research alternatives — the personalities of co-workers, the style of practice, and the nature of the work — before accepting employment. The time you invest will certainly pay off: applicants who know what they want are perceived by employers as more powerful and desirable than those who present themselves as indiscriminate in their needs and eager to accept any offer.

Look at career development as a process. Don't expect your first job out of law school to represent the ideal. Chief Judge Patricia McGowan Wald of the U.S. Circuit Court of Appeals, as quoted in the *National Law Journal,* advises that you approach your early years in the profession with patience. "It may take two or three or four years to find your niche out there," she says. "But the search is worth it."

If, after a few years, your first job is just not satisfying, don't give up. Do your best to find positions which help you develop skills that build upon each other, and then move on when you have gained what you intended. In short, guide your career path with planning, and then persist by taking jobs that propel you forward to your ultimate goal.

Appendix Four:
Recommended Resources

FOR MORE INSPIRATION AND ASSISTANCE WITH CAREER EVALUATION

Work with Passion, Nancy Anderson

A book that gets to the heart of the career change process by exploring how you enjoy spending your time and how you can earn a living doing it. Highly recommended as a self-assessment tool. Paperback; Carroll & Graf and Whatever Publishing, 1984, $8.95.

The 1991 What Color is Your Parachute? A Practical Manual for Job-Hunters & Career Changers, Richard Nelson Bolles

The "Bible" of career change. Good for those who can never get enough data before they make a decision. Annually updated. Paperback; Ten Speed Press, 1991, $11.95.

The Three Boxes of Life (And How to Get Out of Them), Richard Bolles

Who says you have to go to school until age 25, be a lawyer until age 65, and then have fun? Not author Richard Bolles. A wonderful new perspective on the life and work planning process. Paperback; Ten Speed Press, 1978, 1981, $14.95.

Guerrilla Tactics in the Job Market, Tom Jackson

A good career planning guide for the take-charge, goal-oriented reader. Paperback; Bantam Books, 1978, $4.50.

You Can Have It All: The Art of Winning the Money Game and Living a Life of Joy, Arnold Patent

A lawyerly explanation of the way the world works. The author, a former practicing attorney, explains how you can be supported financially by doing what you love for a living. Paperback; Celebration Publishing, 1984, 1988, $10.00.

Wishcraft: How to Get What You Really Want, Barbara Sher

A good, practical, thoroughly motivating guide to defining and achieving your goals. The title may draw skepticism, but the information is superb. Paperback; Ballantine Books, 1979, $6.95.

Do What You Love, The Money Will Follow, Marsha Sinetar

An intellectual explanation of the philosophy behind *Work with Passion*. Not much help with the mechanics of job change, but very well-written, instructive and inspirational. Paperback; Paulist Press, 1987, $7.95.

FOR MORE INFORMATION ABOUT THE JOB-FINDING PROCESS

The Complete Job-Search Handbook, Howard Figler

A practical, clearly written overview of the job-hunting process. The author quickly gets to the bottom of career evaluation and planning, then concentrates mostly on "all the skills you need to get any job and have a good time doing it." Recommended for anyone who has already targeted a type of work or industry, but needs help making contacts and uncovering opportunities. Paperback; Henry Holt, 1979, 1988, $11.95.

The Job Search Handbook: Basics of a Professional Job Search, John Noble

Written by the associate director of career services at Harvard University, this how-to book focuses on securing an executive position by building contacts, letter writing and interviewing, and also covers the negotiation of salary and benefits packages. Paperback; Bob Adams, Inc., 1988, $6.95.

A pamphlet of question-and-answer tips, targeted to jobs in federal government and with private law firms. Available for $3.95 plus $1 postage and handling from Federal Reports, Inc., 1010 Vermont Avenue N.W., Suite 408, Washington, D.C. 10005; (202) 393-3311.

A pamphlet of question-and-answer tips, targeted to jobs in federal government and with private law firms. Available for $3.95 plus $1 postage and handling from Federal Reports, Inc., 1010 Vermont Avenue N.W., Suite 408, Washington, D.C. 10005; (202) 393-3311.

EXPLORING ALTERNATIVES IN THE LEGAL PROFESSION

Lawyers In Transition: Planning a life in the law, MarkByers, Don Samuelson and Gordon Williamson

A career planning workbook designed especially for lawyers. Although it focuses on finding suitable employment within the profession, the exercises can lead you into non-legal careers as well. Includes an excellent list of resources at the end. Paperback; The Barkley Company, 1988, $18.50.

Changing Jobs: A Handbook for Lawyers, edited by Carol Kanarek

An anthology of articles by various experts on career planning, the job search process, and employment opportunities for experienced lawyers. Focuses on job change within the profession or in law-related fields. Paperback; American Bar Association, 1989, $10.00.

ON THE PSYCHOLOGY OF CHANGE

Transitions: Making Sense of Life's Changes, William Bridges

This book helps identify transitional phases, and explores way to welcome and get through them successfully. Paperback; Addison-Wesley, 1980, $7.95.

Feeling Good: The New Mood Therapy, David D. Burns, M.D.

A clearly written explanation and application of cognitive therapy (a drug-free treatment for depression), based on research by the University of Pennsylvania School of Medicine. Helpful in building self-esteem and getting past the negative self-talk that sabotages so many attempts to change careers. Paperback; Signet, 1980, $4.95.

Burn Out: How to Beat the High Cost of Success, Herbert J. Freudenberger, M.D.

191

This book, through anecdotes and straightforward advice, explores the subject of burnout. Recommended for practitioners who are looking for ways to restore balance to their lives without leaving the legal profession or their current jobs. Paperback; Bantam Books, 1980, $3.95.

The Addictive Organization, Anne Wilson Schaef and Dianne Fassel

The authors define addiction as "any substance or process that has taken over our lives and over which we are powerless." This provocative book provides insight into the ties that bind lawyers to their careers. Hardback; Harper & Row, 1988, $16.95.

When Smart People Fail: Rebuilding Yourself for Success, Carol Hyatt and Linda Gottlieb

Highly readable, this book uses anecdotes to help you see bad decisions or actions, or unfortunate circumstances, as springboards for positive change and growth. Paperback; Penguin, 1987, $7.95.

CAREER COUNSELORS

Career counselors neither select your next career nor find your next job. "They should not represent themselves as the ones with all the answers," says Ava Butler. Instead, they provide assistance in exploring appropriate options, researching the possibilities, preparing resumes and conducting interviews.

Career counseling for lawyers, at least during the initial stages, demands a somewhat different approach than for the public-at-large. Most job and career changers are seeking a higher level of prestige and compensation. Attorneys, on the other hand, often want to discard, or at least de-emphasize, their professional identity, and may move into a field that offers less money and prestige. Some attorneys have encountered career counselors who spend too much valuable time encouraging them to override their intuition, and to stick with their legal careers. Sessions with these counselors ended up merely postponing what turned out to be an inevitable and otherwise satisfying career change. Thus, look for counselors who understand the unique issues faced by lawyers, and who display no judgments about your choice to leave the law.

Finding the right career counselor requires the same investigative skills you would recommend others use to locate a good attorney. First, obtain referrals from friends or reputable referral agencies. Next, check credentials and interview the counselor to determine whether his or her personality and approach works well with your own. Finally, avoid counselors who charge a non-refundable flat fee for their services. Instead, work with a counselor who lets you choose the services you desire, and permits you to terminate services at any time, paying only for those services already rendered.

To receive, free of charge, a list of certified career counselors in your geographic area, contact the National Board of Certified Counselors, 5999 Stevenson Avenue, Alexandria, VA 22034. For a listing of reputable career resource centers, write Catalyst, 14 East 60th Street, New York, NY 10022.

TESTING

Johnson O'Connor Research Foundation

Established in 1939, the Johnson-O'Connor Human Engineering Laboratory is the nation's oldest center for the study of human aptitudes. Although anyone can learn to handle difficult tasks, the O'Connor Foundation asserts that true job satisfaction depends on using those aptitudes (or natural talents and skills) with which you were born. Testing takes a day and a half (at $450) and yields a useful and individualized job profile. Offices are located in Atlanta, Boston, Chicago, Dallas/Fort Worth, Denver, Houston, Los Angeles, New Orleans, New York City, Philadelphia, San Diego, San Francisco, Seattle, Tampa, and Washington, D.C.

Myers-Briggs Type Indicator (MBTI)

The *MBTI* is a personality evaluator that studies four sets of character traits, and draws conclusions about an individual's preferences based on the resulting combination. According to Larry Richard, a former lawyer who now relies heavily on the Myers-Briggs in counseling attorneys, the crucial difference between happy and unhappy lawyers is that some are "thinkers" and others are "feelers." Lawyers are trained to be "thinkers," making objective decisions on the basis of cause and effect, and by analyzing and weighing the evidence. Lawyers with a temperamental preference for "feeling," however, prefer to make decisions based on person-centered values, and work to create harmony. These practitioners find it frustrating to solve problems by arguing intellectually about them, and also dislike working in the inherently conflict-ridden environment of the adversarial system. For information about licensed MPTI administrators in your area, contact Consulting Psychologists Press, 3803 East Bayshore Blvd., P. O. Box 10096, Palo Alto, CA 94306; (415) 969-8608 or (800) 624-1765.

Gifts Differing, Isabel Briggs-Myers

An explanation of the Briggs-Myers Type Indicator by one of its creators. Paperback; Consulting Psychologists Press, Inc., 1980, $12.50.

Please Understand Me: Character and Temperament Types, David Kiersey and Marilyn Bates

The authors have devised a simplified version of the MBTI to come up with a "temperament sorter." They apply these personality types, identical to the Myers-Briggs, to preferences in employment, mating, parenting, leadership, and learning. Paperback; Prometheus Nemesis, 1982, $11.95.

Type Talk: The 16 Personality Types that Determine How We Live, Love and Work, Otto Kroeber and Janet M. Thuesen

Another interpretation of the MBTI written in an entertaining, anecdotal fashion. Paperback; Delta, 1988, $9.95.

Strong Interest Inventory
Career Occupational Preference Evaluation (COPS)

Both the *Strong* and *COPS* tests identify interests, as opposed to aptitudes or personality proclivities. The *Strong* targets specific jobs while *COPS* suggests general areas of employment. For example, *Strong* might isolate "mortician" as an ideal job. For the same person, *COPS* would provide a gradation of twelve categories of employment with technical, business, and social skills heading the list. Administered by career counselors and other career planning services nationwide.

194

FOOTNOTES

CHAPTER 1: PRISON UNREST

1. Jones, *The Big Switch: New Careers, New Lives After 35*, McGraw Hill, 1980. Jones based her conclusions on a review of 1970 U.S. Census Bureau statistics which also showed that 33% of all economists and 40% of social workers had changed careers.

2. Reidinger, "The Money Makers," *ABA Journal*, August 1, 1987. According to this survey, 41% of all lawyers still hold their first job in the profession; 29% are in their second. The *Harvard Career Paths Study* (cited below), however, indicated that 22% of the class of 1959 still held their first jobs, while 17% had moved to a second. For the class of 1969, 49% had worked in two different jobs since they graduated from law school.

3. Jackson, *Guerrilla Tactics in the Job Market*, Bantam Books, 1978. In *The Encyclopedia of Second Careers*, Facts on File Publications, 1984, the author, Gene Hawes, says that about 12% of the U.S. work force changes careers every year.

4. Vogt, "From Law School to Career: Where Do Graduates Go and What Do They Do?" *A Career Paths Study of Seven Northeastern Law Schools*, May, 1986 (hereinafter referred to as *Harvard Career Paths Study*). For the Class of 1981, more than half of those who started out working for legal services were still in that job four years later. For all other types of employment, however, the average amount of time in the first position was about 2.5 years.

5. Lacayo, "Rattling the Gilded Cage," *Time*, August 11, 1986. Another source reported that firms are losing up to a third of each year's

class. See Weston, "The Economics of Recruiting, *California Lawyer*, July, 1988.

6.   *Harvard Career Paths Study.*

7.   Hirsch, "Are You On Target?" *Barrister*, Winter, 1985. The overall percentage broke down as follows: 10% of those who report being very satisfied with their current employment, a fifth of those who are somewhat dissatisfied, and 30% of those who feel neutrally about their current jobs. (That survey also showed a 16% overall dissatisfaction rate, with another 17% reporting that they neither liked nor disliked their jobs.)

8.   *Id.*; "A Look at Today's Lawyer," *ABA Journal*, September 1, 1986; Hirsch, "Are You on Target?" *Barrister*, Winter, 1985.

9.   Hirsch, "Are You on Target?," *Barrister*, Winter, 1985. Among partners, 15% of the women and nine percent of the men were dissatisfied. Among senior associates, the figures were 25% for women versus 13% for men. For junior associates, 40% of the women to 19% of the men. Only for solo practitioners was the discrepancy minor: 18% of the men to 21% of the women.

10.   Smith, "A Profile of Lawyer Lifestyles," *ABA Journal*, February, 1984. An earlier survey administered by the Young Lawyers Division of the American Bar Association concluded that 40% of all young lawyers were dissatisfied with their jobs. Munneke and Bridger-Riley, "Singing Those Law Office Blues," *Barrister*, Spring, 1980. Because of the gravity of its implications, a second survey was commissioned in 1983. That survey showed a 25% dissatisfaction rate among junior associates and staff attorneys. Hirsch, "Are You on Target?" *Barrister*, Winter, 1985.

11.   Barron, "Malaise Among Maryland Lawyers," *The New York Times*, January 27, 1989. Eighty percent cited negative public opinion about lawyers as a cause of their dissatisfaction. Almost all were concerned that law is becoming less of a profession and more of a business than it used to be.

CHAPTER 2: THE SCENE OF THE CRIME

1.   Hirsch, "Are You On Target?" *Barrister*, Winter, 1985. One quarter of those surveyed intended to change jobs in the next two years, 31% of them outside of law. There are approximately 723,000 practicing attorneys according to the January, 1988, U.S. Department of Labor, Bureau of Labor Statistics. That calculates to 28,016 attorneys looking for jobs outside the legal profession. Documentation of the number of lawyers who are actually leaving the law, however, is difficult to find. For example, as of 1970, according to Jones, *The Big Switch: New Careers, New Lives After 35*, McGraw Hill, 1980, only six percent of practicing lawyers ever left the profession. Fifteen years later, the *Harvard Career Paths Study* reported that 13% of all law school graduates held non-legal positions (nearly 20% of the class of 1959). Although this might appear to be a doubling of the numbers withdrawing from the profession, it is unclear whether Jones included in her statistics those law school graduates who never practiced law. And, the Harvard statistics include in their definition of law-related positions some which might be defined as non-legal — law firm administrators, law enforcement officials, government contract officers, trainers and full-time lobbyists.

2.   Smith, "A Profile of Lawyer Lifestyles," *ABA Journal*, February, 1984. The article stated that 59% reported that they would again choose law as a career if they had the past to relive.

3.   Nabbefeld, "No Rest for the Weary," *California Lawyer*, January, 1989.

4.   Lefer, "Attorneys Are Among Most Severely Stressed Groups," *New York Law Journal*, September 29, 1986.

5.   WSBA Lawyers' Assistance Program Staff, "Are Lawyers Distressed? . . . And How?!" *Washington State Bar News*, February, 1988.

6.   According to the American Bar Association, 12 to 15% of all lawyers nationwide are addicted to alcohol. "One Lawyer's Triumph Over Alcohol," *ABA Journal*, December 1, 1987. The Washington State Bar Association survey, however, referred to in the preceding note, concluded that 18% of their members abused alcohol, as compared to

the reported national average of 10%.

7.   Some of the statements in this profile were originally printed in the April, 1985, issue of the *Seattle-King County Bar Bulletin*, and in the February, 1988, issue of *Trial News*, the official publication of the Washington State Trial Lawyers Association.

8.   Celebration Publishing.

9.   The population of lawyers increased from 326,000 in 1970 to 676,000 in 1987. Reidinger, "The Money Makers," *ABA Journal*, August 1, 1987. The U.S. population increased 17.6% in that same time period. *Statistical Abstract of the U.S., 1987*, U.S. Department of Commerce, Bureau of the Census.

10.   "The Changing of the Guard," May 15, 1987.

11.   American Bar Association, 1988.

12.   Reed, "Value Billing," *Legal Economics*, September, 1988.

13.   Cobb, "Competitive Pricing," *Legal Economics*, September, 1988.

14.   Labaton, "Law Firm Incomes Surging on Deals and Tax Work," *The New York Times*, July 5, 1988. Average income for partners at the 15 most profitable law firms nationwide was $739,000. Partners at Wachtell, Lipton, Rosen & Katz reported the highest per partner profits, averaging $1.4 million. The median income of all lawyers nationwide in 1987, according to the ABA, was $68,922.

15.   Moss, "There's a PC on My Desk," *ABA Journal*, October 1, 1988. Law firm management consulting firm Altman & Weil says the legal profession is experiencing a "profit squeeze" as partner incomes fail to keep pace with the rate of inflation. From 1977 to 1987, average partner compensation increased by 63% while the cost of living increased by 100%. An increase of 114% in average gross receipts was more than negated by a 153% rise in overhead, excluding associate salaries. (Associate salaries increased by only 80%.)

16.   Reidinger, "Still Got Something to Say," May 15, 1987.

17.   Harper, "The Best and Brightest, Bored and Burned Out," *ABA Journal*, May 15, 1987.

CHAPTER 3: THE RUNNER'S PROFILE

1. "Those #*X Lawyers," *Time*, April 10, 1978.

2. Hirsch, "Are You On Target?" *Barrister*, Winter, 1985. More than half of those lawyers surveyed worked in excess of eight hours per day. Forty percent were dissatisfied with the amount of vacation time. In another survey, the average ABA member reportedly bills 47 hours each week in addition to two hours of civic or pro bono work and over three hours commuting. In addition, 83% reportedly work at least one Saturday, and 57% at least one Sunday, every month. Smith, "A Profile of Lawyer Lifestyles," *ABA Journal*, February, 1984. And still a third poll determined that the average lawyer worked a 50-hour week; only 13% worked 40 hours per week or less. "Law Poll," *ABA Journal*, October, 1984.

3. Greenhouse, "Linowitz's Call for Lawyers to Be People Again," *The New York Times*, April 22, 1988.

4. In "A Profile of Lawyer Lifestyles," referenced above, 57% of those surveyed cited more time for a personal life as the most desired improvement in their working environment. In "Are You On Target?" also referenced above, more time for family was the most frequently cited request. "A Look at Today's Lawyer," *ABA Journal*, September, 1986, stated that the typical lawyer is a hard working entrepreneur who would like to spend more time with his family.

5. "Cooling Out," December, 1986.

6. "Women and the Law," *Ms.*, June, 1987.

7. *Id.*, and U.S. Department of Labor, Bureau of Labor Statistics, January, 1988.

8. Smith, "A Profile of Lawyer Lifestyles," *ABA Journal*, February, 1984; "Women and the Law," *Ms.*, June, 1987. In the October, 1983, *ABA Journal*, the figures were even more skewed. 32% of all female attorneys have never married as compared to only eight percent of the men. 46% of the women were unmarried as compared to 15% of the men.

9. Fowler, "Difficulties for Women Lawyers," *The New York Times*, January 24, 1989.

10. The term "win/win" refers to an approach to deal-making and problem solving in which the belief prevails that both sides can get what they need; in other words, that both sides win from the agreement. For

a good explanation of the "win/win" concept, read Fisher and Ury, *GETTING TO YES: Negotiating Agreement Without Giving In*, Houghton Mifflin Company, 1981, Penguin Books, 1983, and Fisher and Brown, *GETTING TOGETHER: Building a Relationship that Gets to YES*, Houghton Mifflin Company, 1988.

11. In a "win/lose" approach to problem solving, one side prevails at the expense of the other. This is the general philosophy of the adversarial system. Sometimes, however, neither side prevails, especially when a judge reaches a decision and orders a remedy that doesn't take either side's needs into consideration, and comes at a high economic and emotional cost for them both. Then, a "lose/lose" result occurs.

12. Reskin, "A Portrait of America's Law Students," *ABA Journal*, May, 1985.

13. Burke, "Lawyers — The Non-Practitioners," *Rhode Island Bar Journal*, December, 1984.

14. Nolo Press.

CHAPTER 4: UP AGAINST THE WALL

1.   Smith, "A Profile of Lawyer Lifestyles," *ABA Journal*, February, 1984. The statistics cited in this article were from a survey made in May, 1983. During the interim six years, rapid changes in the professional climate have probably led to higher levels of dissatisfaction and of flight. In fact, a 1988 Maryland Bar Association survey indicated that a third of the membership was planning to leave the profession. And, in December, 1988, a lecturer at a Seattle continuing legal education seminar on office management asked the large audience of practitioners how many would not again choose law as a career. By his estimate, well over half of those in the room raised their hands.

2.   Hirsch, "Are You On Target?" *Barrister*, Winter, 1985. Twenty-five percent of all those surveyed in the ABA's 1984 survey of the profession were planning to change jobs in the next two years. Of them, 31% were looking outside of the legal profession. That translates to 7.75% of all lawyers.

3.   "Among Career Choices, a Booming Year in Law," *The New York Times*, June 1, 1988. And the upward trend has continued. The Law

School Admissions Council reported that applications for the 1989-90 academic year increased 22% over those for 1988-89. "Law School Applicants Up," *The New York Times*, March 3, 1989.

4. *Harvard Career Paths Study.*

5. Starting salaries for the top 10% of all law school graduates, as of the Fall, 1988, entering class, were reportedly $71,000. "A Salary Pinch for this Year's Law Grad," *The National Law Journal*, May 30, 1988. Many public interest positions pay under $25,000 annually. "The 14th Annual Salary Survey," *Student Lawyer*, November, 1988; Keaton, "Paying a Debt to Society," *California Lawyer*, October, 1988.

6. "Aimless Associates," *American Lawyer*, October, 1987.

7. Weston, "The Economics of Recruiting: it can take three years for a new lawyer to earn the costs of hiring him," *California Lawyer*, July, 1988.

8. *Id.*

9. Monkman, "Courting Recruits: Law firms become a "party" to suit," *Seattle Post-Intelligencer*, June 27, 1988.

10. Brill, "Aimless Associates," *American Lawyer*, October, 1987.

11. As told to Linda Kerr Stores, principal of Seattle's Kerr Stores Legal Search.

12. Biehl, January, 1989.

13. Harper, "The Best and Brightest, Bored and Burned Out," *ABA Journal*, May 15, 1987.

14. Trager, "The lawyers who hate practicing law," *San Francisco Examiner*, December 22, 1985. Since most non-practitioners maintain their bar memberships after they stop practicing law, a simple review of the numbers of attorneys who have let their bar association memberships lapse cannot paint an accurate picture of the numbers withdrawing from the profession. And, relying upon the inactive membership rolls is equally distorting. First, those figures could reflect mobility, that is, the rate at which lawyers are crossing state lines to find employment, more than abandonment of the profession. And, many attorneys who are inactive members of one bar association are actively practicing in another jurisdiction.

CHAPTER 5: MAKING THE BREAK

1. Bower, "Young and Restless; Lawyers Who Leave," *Barrister*, Summer, 1986.

CHAPTER 6: ASSUMING A NEW IDENTITY

1. *Seattle Post-Intelligencer*, October 18, 1988.

2. "Among Career Choices, a Booming Year in Law," *The New York Times*, June 1, 1988; "Law School Applications Take Off," *California Lawyer*, April, 1988.

3. Harper, "The Best and Brightest, Bored and Burned Out," *ABA Journal*, May 15, 1987.

4. Natale, "Going Hollywood," *California Lawyer*, September, 1987.

5. Hanley, "Money, Power Lure Lawyers to Investment Banks," *L.A. Daily Journal*, July 17, 1987.

6. Redd, "Many Lawyers Now Finding Their Practices Aren't Perfect," *Newsday*, July 21, 1986.

7. Hanley, "Money, Power Lure Lawyers to Investment Banks," *L.A. Daily Journal*, July 17, 1987.

8. Lawhorn, "Making Changes," *The Orange County Register*, July 26, 1987.

9. Jones, "Leavitt uses wit to win friends and influence people," *Puget Sound Business Journal*, February 22, 1988.

10. Zeitlin, "Mid-Life Career Changes," *The Jewish Journal*, March 4-10, 1988.

11. "Lawyers As Entrepreneurs, *NYU Law*, Spring, 1986.

12. New American Libraries, 1984.

13. Redd, "Many Lawyers Now Finding Their Practices Aren't Perfect, *Newsday*, July 21, 1986.

14. Wise, "Doing the Write Thing," *National Law Journal*, January 20, 1986.

15. Bower, "Young and Restless; Lawyers Who Leave," *Barrister*, Summer, 1986.

16. Zeitlin, "Mid-Life Career Changes," *The Jewish Journal*, March 4-10, 1988.

17. Harper, "The Best and Brightest, Bored and Burned Out," *ABA Journal*, May 15, 1987.

18. Natale, "Going Hollywood," *California Lawyer*, September, 1987.

19. Natale, "From Boston law to 'L.A. Law,'" *California Lawyer*, September, 1987.

20. Natale, "Going Hollywood," *California Lawyer*, September, 1987.

21. Berger, "Allure of Teaching Revival: Education School Rolls Surge," *The New York Times*, May 6, 1988.

22. Uni*Sun, 1989.

23. Anderson, "A new life in the slow lane," *Seattle Post-Intelligencer*, August 17, 1986.

CHAPTER EIGHT: COPING WITHIN THE LAW

1. Stindt, "An 80% Solution Is Not Realistic," *California Lawyer*, April, 1988.

2. And now, many large law firms (especially in the East) are abandoning their sabbatical programs in favor of working harder than ever. Nabbefeld, "No Rest for the Weary: sabbaticals for partners are fast disappearing," *California Lawyer*, January, 1989.

3. Harper & Row, 1988.

CHAPTER NINE: REHABILITATING THE SYSTEM

1. Hirsch, "Are You On Target?" *Barrister*, Winter, 1985.

2. Harper & Row, 1988. Additional characteristics of an addictive organization include confusion, self-centeredness, dishonesty, perfectionism, control, disconnection from feelings, ethical deterioration, a crisis orientation, depression, stress, forgetfulness, dependency, negativism, defensiveness, projection, tunnel vision, and fear. When organi-

zations continue to function addictively, they will exacerbate their existing problems and develop more complex, destructive problems; become less moral and ethical, and more ruthless; lose their influence; and eventually "bottom out" just like any drunk.

3. Tolman, "Let's Ban Billing by the Hour," *Legal Economics*, September, 1988.

4. Feferman, "Motivating Your Associates," *ABA Journal*, February, 1989.

5. Margolick, "At the Bar," *The New York Times*, September 30, 1988.

6. Margolick, "At the Bar," *The New York Times*, July 22, 1988. However, even this firm's efforts at humanizing the office environment are beginning to erode. Some partners are now complaining that the annual critique process is too time-consuming, humiliating and unreliable and a disappointing movement is afoot to abandon this annual attempt at self-evaluation.

7. Benjamin, Kaszniak, Sales & Shanfield, "The Role of Legal Education in Producing Psychological Distress Among Law Students and Lawyers," *American Bar Foundation Research Journal*, Spring, 1986.

8. Cramton, "The Trouble with Lawyers (And Law Schools)," *Journal of Legal Education*, September, 1985.

9. Greenhouse, "Linowitz's Call for Lawyers to Be People Again," *The New York Times*, April 22, 1988.

10. Moss, "Law Firm Role Models," *ABA Journal*, October 1, 1988.

11. "ABA recommends creeds for bar associations," *ABA Journal*, January, 1989.

12. Sayler, *ABA Journal*, March 1, 1988.

13. Fisher and Ury, Houghton Mifflin Company (1981), Penguin Books (1983).

14. "Making Lawsuits Better for Everyone," a speech delivered to benefit the Charles & Annie Goldmark Foundation, Seattle, Washington, May 1, 1986.

15. Raven and Koniak, "The Challenge for Lawyers in the 90's," *California Lawyer*, August, 1987.

APPENDIX 1: CAREER PLANNING TIPS FOR DISSATISFIED LAWYERS

1. Kolata, "Secret of Surviving Mid-Career Malaise: Just Work Elsewhere," *The New York Times*, January, 1989.

2. Slade, "Law Degree Wanes as Passport to Business Job," *The New York Times*, January 27, 1989.